THE OFFICIAL

All My Children
TRIVIA BOOK

THE OFFICIAL
All My
Children
TRIVIA BOOK

GERARD J. WAGGETT

NEW YORK

Library of Congress Cataloging-in-Publication Data

Waggett, Gerard J.
    The official All my children trivia book / by Gerard J. Waggett.
— 1st ed.
p. cm.
    ISBN 0-7868-8283-2
    1. All my children (Television program)—Miscellanea. I. Title.
PN1992.77.A5W28 1998
791.45'72—dc21   97-40011
                                                                CIP

DESIGNED BY MICHELLE BONOMO

FIRST EDITION

10 9 8 7 6 5 4 3 2 1

For my editors at *Soap Opera Weekly*,
Freeman, Mimi, Irene, and Jonathan

ACKNOWLEDGMENTS

As always, my first debt of thanks goes to my editor, Gretchen Young. I still remember that day before Thanksgiving when you called to say you wanted me to write this *All My Children* trivia book as well as the one on *General Hospital*. That phone call started my holiday season off on just the right note. To my agents, Frank Coffey and Frank Weimann, my continued thanks for your encouragement, advice, and help. To Gail Silverman and Sandra Dorsey at ABC, once again thank you for locating the pictures I needed. And Jennifer Lang, you've been great handling all the varied problems I've thrown at you.

My parents, Barbara and Fred Waggett, continue to be a source of support and encouragement. For their role in the overall picture, I would like to thank them along with my aunt Margaret, my uncles Jackie and Eddie Connolly, my cousin Mabel Waggett, my brother Michael and his wife Christine, my brother Kevin, my brother Freddy and his wife Keri, my nieces, Norma, Taylor, and Ava, and my friends Eileen Maher, Don Casali, and Jamie Walsh. For making his computer and printer so accessible, I have to thank Dennis Coughlin. And for their insight into the world of daytime television and their feedback on this book, I have to thank Scott Reedy and Louise Shaffer.

My writing career, I should add, really started moving ahead while I was freelancing for *Soap Opera Weekly*. The first editor there to give me the go-ahead on an article was

Freeman Günter. For that I will be forever grateful. Because of him and his fellow editors—Irene Keene, Jonathan Reiner, and editor in chief Mimi Torchin—I've been able to interview some of daytime's biggest stars, a number of them from *All My Children:* Marcy Walker, Robin Mattson, Walt Willey, Teresa Blake, and Susan Lucci as well as Agnes Nixon herself. The magazine also allowed me the opportunity to talk with such famous *All My Children* fans as Luther Vandross, Kate Pierson from the B-52s, and Nichelle Nichols from *Star Trek.* I owe my editors at *Soap Opera Weekly* many thanks and a couple of apologies for the articles that I still haven't turned in. I could tell you that they're coming, but you probably know better by now.

CONTENTS

INTRODUCTION

When I was a junior in college, Agnes Nixon came to Harvard to receive a humanitarian award and talk to the students about writing for daytime. Like so many of the other students who showed up that afternoon, I wasn't looking just for career advice. I wanted to meet the woman who had built Pine Valley, the woman who had given birth to Erica Kane and Palmer Cortlandt. All of us that day came armed with questions about the show: Is Greg going to find Jenny's letter before she marries Tony Barclay? Who's stashed away in Adam Chandler's attic? And, of course, Is Susan Lucci anything like Erica Kane? Nixon didn't dodge that last question; she assured us that Susan was as nice as Erica was spoiled.

A lot of people who attend Nixon's talk had gotten into *All My Children* when they started college, but I had about a year's head start on them. During my senior year of high school, my class schedule ended every Friday at 12:30. At my school, once your classes were done for the day, you were free to go home. If my uncle picked me up, I could be sitting down in front of the TV set with my lunch before that mysterious hand opened the photo album.

It was all the mystery surrounding Cortlandt Manor that drew me into *All My Children*. During *General Hospital*, I'd seen the promos where Myra Murdoch and Nina Cortlandt were conducting a seance to contact the ghost of Nina's mother. The *Dark Shadows* fan inside me had to

Palmer Cortlandt's masquerade ball. 1980/Steve Fenn

check out a story line like that. And, of course, I wanted to see for myself what the deal was with this "Erica" person who people were always talking about.

A couple of Friday afternoons was all it took for me to add *All My Children* to my afternoon lineup. It has remained that way for seventeen years and counting. Collected here are some of the episodes, scenes, and story lines that have left the biggest impression on me:

Palmer's masquerade ball (1980). Palmer's first wife Daisy came back from "the dead" at his masquerade ball, and Palmer chased after her with his hounds. This was pure gothic drama.

Donna's pregnancy (1982). When his wife Donna announced that she was pregnant, Palmer knew the child wasn't his. A polo accident had rendered him sterile (a condition which has since reversed itself). Palmer paid a sleazy doctor to tell Donna that her baby would be born with severe birth defects. Palmer then convinced the distraught Donna that an abortion would be the best course of action. While the plan failed because of Donna's ex, Chuck Tyler, the baby's father, the storyline cemented Palmer as the show's most fascinating villain.

Jenny and Jesse's summer in New York (1982). Daytime fell in love with Jenny Gardner and Greg Nelson as a couple, but the more interesting relationship was the near angelic Jenny's friendship with the street-tough Jesse Hubbard. After Liza Colby told Jenny that her father was a rapist and accused Jesse of attempted rape, Jesse and Jenny hid out in New York for the summer. The writers gave their growing friendship the same sort of attention usually saved for romantic couples.

The Erica/Kent/Silver triangle (1983). Once Erica's mousy half-sister Silver let down her hair and threw on some makeup and a pair of heels, you knew she was headed for Kent's bed. And as soon as Erica started talking about buying an antique gun for Kent, you knew this triangle was going to end up with someone getting killed. But the writers still had one surprise waiting: Silver Kane was an impostor.

The Liza/Tad/Marian triangle (1983). When Tad Martin two-timed his girlfriend Liza Colby with her own mother, he performed two small miracles. Not only did he get away with it for months before either woman caught on, he actually made the audience feel sympathy for Liza Colby. The reverberations from that triangle are still being felt fifteen years later.

Devon's same-sex crush (1983). More than a few jaws dropped when Devon McFadden's new friend Dr. Lynn Carson came out to her. Lynn was the first lesbian character to hit daytime. Unlucky-with-men Devon developed a crush on Lynn and suggested that they begin a physical relationship. Although Lynn turned Devon down, Devon's suggestion was a bold move for a major soap character.

Tad and Dottie (1984). As hard as it was for Tad to sink any lower after the Liza/Marian affair, he cemented his reputation as town cad by taking money from nouveauriche Edna Ferguson to date her insecure, overweight daughter Dottie.

Erica's screen test (1984). One of daytime's funniest scenes, Erica auditioned to play herself in the film version of her autobiography. Erica re-created the scene where she confronted her "half sister Silver" with a gun. "Did you sleep with him?" Erica demanded to know. "Yes?" she asked, nodding the barrel of the gun up and down, "Or no?" she added, shaking the barrel side to side. Erica was so bad, she didn't get the role playing herself even after marrying the film's producer, Adam Chandler, but Lucci showed off a gift for physical comedy.

Mark's AIDS scare (1987). The show pulled off an incredible Friday cliffhanger when ex-drug addict Mark Dalton learned that Fred Parker, an old acquaintance of his, had died of an AIDS-related disease. As the show closed, Mark remembered having once shared a needle with Fred at a shooting gallery. *All My Children* was one of the first soaps to deal with AIDS, and the fact that a longtime character like Mark Dalton might be affected drove the point home.

Cindy and Stuart's romance (1987–89). While Mark tested negative, Fred's widow Cindy wasn't so lucky. Through Cindy Parker, the writers educated the audience about safe sex and tolerance. The real highlight of Cindy's story was her romance with Adam Chandler's simple minded but artistic twin Stuart. Although Stuart may have seemed like an odd choice of character around whom to build one of daytime's first AIDS stories, it paid off. The childlike innocence of Stuart and of Cindy allowed a beautifully touching romance to flourish under extremely dire circumstances.

Kendall's revenge (1992–94). Erica has racked up almost as many adversaries over the years as she has husbands (Natalie, Brooke, Barbara, Maria, et cetera). The most intriguing of these was her own daughter Kendall, a child conceived during a rape and given up for adoption at birth. The chemistry between Erica and Kendall was compelling. Kendall both hated and worshipped her mother while Erica tried to be a mother to a child she simply couldn't accept. When Kendall sabotaged Erica's wedding to Dimitri, she was just getting started on an almost Satanic course of revenge. Kendall accused Erica's husband Dimitri of raping her and later brought to town her rapist father.

Erica's testimony (1994). If I had to pick the one scene that should have won Susan Lucci her Emmy, I would have chosen the day she took the witness stand during her attempted murder trial. Believing Kendall's lie that Dimitri had raped her, Erica had flipped out and stabbed her husband. She had envisioined him as Richard Fields, the man who had raped her as a child. In an effort to build a defense on temporary insanity, Erica took the stand and recounted the horror of being raped at the age of fourteen. While Lucci has long played Erica larger than life, she talked about being powerless, pointing out "I'm not a big person," with an understated vulnerability that was painful to hear. Ironically, this was the year that Lucci wasn't even nominated for the Best Actress Emmy. The show intercut Erica's testimony with a scene in which Richard Fields cornered Erica's daughter Bianca in his hotel room. The juxtaposition was downright chilling.

Seems my whole life waits on hold for Erica.

—Urge Overkill, "Erica Kane"

THE OFFICIAL

All My Children

TRIVIA BOOK

The
All My Children
Time Line

1965: Agnes Nixon completed her proposal for *All My Children* in 1965 during a family vacation on the island of Saint Croix. The suitcase containing the only copy of Nixon's proposal was lost en route back to the United States and was missing for several weeks.

All My Children creator Agnes Nixon. 1981/Steve Fenn

1967: Agnes Nixon went to work as head writer on Procter & Gamble's *Another World*. While there, she created the character of Rachel Davis (originated by Robin Strasser). Rachel had grown up poor with an absentee father and saw marriage into a wealthy family as her ticket out of poverty.

1968: The character of Rachel Davis was part of a pivotal love triangle that not only saved *Another World* from cancellation but propelled the soap to number two in the ratings. That ratings surge caught the attention of ABC, which then approached Nixon about creating a soap opera for the network. Because Procter & Gamble had passed on *All My Children*, Nixon created a new soap opera for ABC, *One Life to Live*, which debuted on July 15.

1969: Happy with *One Life to Live*'s success, ABC came back to Nixon and asked her for another soap. It was then, and with her husband's encouragement, that Nixon dug out the *All My Children* proposal. ABC loved the idea, especially the young love story Nixon had outlined, a triangle among Tara Martin, Phil Brent, and Chuck Tyler. ABC had been looking for a soap opera that would draw in young viewers. Nixon recruited two actresses with whom she had worked on *As the World Turns*: Ruth Warrick, who had played the adulterous Edith Hughes, and Rosemary Prinz, who had risen to popularity as daytime's first teen heroine, Penny Hughes. Ironically, Nixon wanted Prinz for the role of Amy Tyler, mother to the show's teen hero, Phil Brent.

1970: *All My Children*, which premiered on January 5, 1970, was the first soap opera to debut in the '70s. Three other soap operas debuted that year: *Best of Everything*, based on the Rona Jaffe novel and Joan Crawford film; *A World Apart*, based on the life of Agnes Nixon's mentor Irna Phillips; and *Somerset*, a spin-off from *Another World*, the soap Agnes Nixon had popularized in the late '60s.

1970: Many of the performers on *All My Children*, including Susan Lucci herself, started off with a ten-day pickup clause in their contracts. After ten days, the actors could be fired for any reason. Four key roles were recast during the first year: Lincoln Tyler, Ann Tyler, Kate Martin, and Jeff Martin. Kate and Ann were both recast twice during that first year.

1970–73: *All My Children* did not start out strong in its ratings. Its first year on the air, it ranked seventeenth out

All My Children's original teen couple, Phil and Tara (Richard Hatch and Karen Lynn Gorney). pre-1980/ABC

of nineteen soaps. Its second year it ranked seventeenth out of eighteen soaps. The year after that it ranked seventeenth out of seventeen soaps. However, while its ranking remained uniform, its audience was building with each passing year.

1972: The drafting of Phil Brent (Richard Hatch) was a monumental plot twist for the Phil-Tara-Chuck triangle. In real life, the draft ended almost immediately after the show was taped but before the episode aired. By that time, it was too late for the story to be rewritten or the episodes retaped to catch up with the real world.

1973: During the story line in which Erica develops a potentially fatal infection after having an abortion, the switchboard at ABC lit up with calls from doctors and nurses, offering their medical opinions on how best to treat Erica's case.

1975: In an effort to make the transition from Chris Hubbell to Richard Van Vleet as Chuck Tyler easier for the audience to accept, the show decided that Van Vleet needed to have his hair lightened, just a few streaks added in. In the process, the hairstylist for the show turned Van Vleet's hair orange. Van Vleet's wife, a beautician, managed to undo the damage. When he tried to let his hair color grow out, the producer sent him back to the same hairstylist, who turned his hair orange once again.

1975: Agnes Nixon sold *All My Children* to ABC in 1975. Up till that point, her company, Creative Horizons, owned the show and packaged it for the network. The network supplied the sets, the studios, the costume designers, et cetera, while Creative Horizons supplied the producers, writers, directors, and performers. Rising production costs prompted Nixon's decision to sell.

1975: Agnes Nixon first experimented with the hour format. ABC gave newcomer *Ryan's Hope All My Children*'s time slot. To help the *All My Children* audience make the transition to tuning in a half hour earlier each day, a week before *Ryan's Hope* was to premiere, *All My Children* was pushed back into a new time slot and expanded to an hour for the week.

1977: In January of 1977, *All My Children* and *Ryan's Hope* switched time slots, sending *All My Children* back to its original starting time. There it stayed for the next twenty years and counting.

1977: In April, *All My Children* expanded to a full hour. Agnes Nixon had not wanted the increase. She worried that the expansion would result in padded scripts and a poorer product. Some of the actors had even threatened to quit if the show went to an hour. ABC, which now owned the show, wanted to fill its afternoon time slot with a known quantity rather than begin another soap opera from scratch. The increase to an hour created the need for more room. ABC therefore broke down the wall between Studio 18, where *All My Children* was taped, and Studio 19, where *One Life to Live* was taped. *One Life to Live*'s sets were displaced to accommodate *All My Children.*

1978–79: *All My Children* overtook *As the World Turns* as the most popular soap opera in the country. *As the World Turns*, which Nixon herself had helped to create, had been daytime's most popular soap for twenty years. The following year, *All My Children* was unseated as the most popular soap by *General Hospital*, which was entering the height of its popularity.

1979: Nicholas Benedict (*Phil Brent*) left *All My Children* in 1979. Although Benedict himself had taken over the role from Richard Hatch, the show decided not to recast. Instead, Phil was killed off a second and final time. The death of Phil, whose romance with Tara had dominated *All My Children* for much of the '70s, brought a symbolic close to the show's first decade. Because Phil was a Vietnam veteran, he received a military funeral. The Ceremonial Guard

Nina Cortlandt and Cliff Warner's (Taylor Miller and Peter Bergman) fairy-tale wedding. 1980/Steve Fenn

from Fort Hamilton in New York officiated over his on-screen burial.

1979: The character of Palmer's housekeeper–mother-in-law Myra Murdoch (Elizabeth Lawrence) was modeled after the Mrs. Danvers character in the Daphne du Maurier novel and Alfred Hitchcock film *Rebecca*.

1980: Cliff and Nina's fairy tale–themed wedding, complete with horse-drawn carriages and exterior filming, set a new standard for daytime nuptials in the '80s.

1981: The plot twist in which Brooke discovers that her drug-dealing mother Peg English (Patricia Barry) was not her biological mother came out of Barry's reluctance to play the scenes in which Peg was plotting Brooke's murder.

Barry could not put herself in the mind-set of a mother planning to kill her own child. She told the producers that the only way she could play the story line would be if it turned out that Brooke was not her daughter but the daughter of her husband's mistress. Brooke and the audience did not discover this until the story's denouement.

1982–84: Daisy Cortlandt's pet cat Bonkers actually belonged to executive producer Jacqueline Babbin. After the cat died in real life, James Mitchell and Gillian Spencer went to an animal shelter to rescue a pair of kittens named Tweedle-Dum and Tweedle-Dee which Palmer would give to Daisy on-screen.

1983: *All My Children* introduced daytime's first lesbian, Dr. Lynn Carson, played by Donna Pescow. While other soaps such as *The Young and the Restless* and *Days of Our Lives* had toyed around with bisexuality, Lynn was the first lesbian character on the soaps. The writers had considered introducing a male homosexual but decided against it because that was already being done on the prime-time serial *Dynasty*. The show took an even more daring turn when a major character, Devon McFadden (Tricia Pursley) developed a same-sex crush on Lynn and approached the subject of making their relationship physical. Lynn declined, explaining to Devon that she was not gay, merely confused after her breakup with Cliff Warner.

1984: During the 1984 Summer Olympics, ABC scrapped the idea of putting all its soaps on hiatus for two weeks and giving rival networks a chance to lure away viewers. While *Ryan's Hope* and *Loving* did take a break, *All My Children* along with *One Life to Live* and *General Hospital* ran abbreviated episodes of forty minutes rather than a full hour.

1988: While pregnant with Bianca, Erica developed toxemia and slipped into a coma. During that coma, Erica envisioned her life as a romantic movie being filmed by her father. The two-day special recapped Erica's life at the major turning point of becoming a mother for what the audience thought was the first time. It was one of the first times a show had dedicated more than one episode to showing old clips. In addition to those clips, the two-day coma dream brought back a number of Erica's former leading men.

1989: After the cancellation of *Ryan's Hope*, ABC decided to see if its New York–produced soap operas wanted any of the sets before they were destroyed. As it turned out, both *All My Children* and *One Life to Live* wanted the set that had been used for Ryan's Bar. The higher-ups decided that the only fair thing to do would be to flip a coin. *One Life to Live* won the bar, which became Max's Place.

1989: Cliff Warner and Nina Cortland set a record for soap opera couples by getting married a fourth time. Many soap opera supercouples have married each other twice, and a few have made it down the aisle together three times. But none aside from Cliff and Nina have married each other four times. Even more impressive, they squeezed all those weddings into one decade, marrying for the first time in 1980 and the fourth time in 1989. Their fourth wedding was considerably less grand than their first, with only immediate family present as witnesses.

Cliff and Nina (Peter Bergman and Taylor Miller) married for a fourth time in 1989. 1989/Ann Limongello

1989: One of the most expensive props the show ever used was the Learjet that crashed with Erica and Jackson on board. Rather than destroy such an expensive plane, a lesser-priced one was crashed for the scenes shot amid the wreckage.

1990: All My Children marked its twentieth anniversary with a special episode that featured the five remaining actors from the original cast: Ray MacDonnell (*Joe Martin*), Mary Fickett (*Ruth Martin*), Ruth Warrick (*Phoebe Tyler Wallingford*), Frances Heflin (*Mona Kane Tyler*), and Susan Lucci (*Erica Kane*). The episode included a number of clips from past episodes. A few of the clips the producers wanted couldn't be used because they featured Walt Willey (*Jackson Montgomery*) from his days as an extra on the show.

1990: In honor of the twentieth anniversary, a new introduction was taped for the show. The hand opening the family photo album, which had begun the show for twenty years, was retired. The new introduction retained the photo album theme, showing framed and loose photographs of the show's various cast members. The opening ended with the photo album closing on a picture of Susan Lucci. While the previous introduction lasted twenty years, this one lasted only five.

1991: Geoffrey Beene designed the wedding dress that Ceara Connor (Genie Francis) wore when she married Jeremy Hunter (Jean LeClerc). Beene's familiarity with *All My Children* and his respect for the show made him break his rule against designing clothes for TV characters.

1991: The hunt for an actor to play Dimitri Marrick took so long that by the time Michael Nader was hired, he was already three weeks behind in his shooting schedules. His first few weeks on the job kept him at work until close to midnight every night.

1993: The patch of quicksand in which Brooke English nearly drowned was actually made up of approximately fifteen thousand pounds of oatmeal mixed with nutmeg and cinnamon.

1993: In one of Ingrid Rogers's (*Taylor Cannon*) most visually intriguing story lines, Taylor went under cover as a Greek heiress to infiltrate Deconstruction, a white racist organization operating on the campus of Pine Valley University. The makeup job that transformed the African-

In 1994, a tornado ripped through Pine Valley (pictured: Eva LaRue, Teresa Blake, Winsor Harmon, and Jill Larson). 1994/Ann Limongello

American Taylor into the white Diana Pappas took approximately two hours per day.

1994: A plastic surgeon was hired to wrap the bandages during the story line in which Janet Green (Robin Mattson) underwent reconstructive surgery on her face. The process took the doctor a solid hour. While authentic looking, the slit holes for the eyes were not wide enough for Mattson to read her script. Christopher Goutman modeled Janet's plastic surgery scene after one of his favorite episodes of *The Twilight Zone.*

1994: In shooting the 1994 tornado scenes, a giant engine was used to generate the seventy-five-mile-an-hour winds. The scenes also required two fans and an air cannon. Ten cameras as opposed to the usual three were used in taping the scenes. Up until the tornado destroyed the Martin house, the set had been the show's oldest one still in use.

1994: In 1994, during Tad's out-of-body experience, Kim Delaney had come back for one day to play his sister Jenny's spirit. Delaney had last been seen on *All My Children* ten years earlier. Also seen in heaven was Darnell Williams as Jesse Hubbard, who had been killed off in 1988.

1995: On the occasion of the twenty-fifth anniversary, the show once again updated its opening sequence. Moving pictures of the show's contract players were set against scenes from around Pine Valley. When the opening premiered, however, the faces of the cast members did not move. The opening alternates each day, with half the cast members shown one day and the other half the next. The one exception is Susan Lucci, a shot of whom begins the opening each day.

1995: In honor of *All My Children*'s twenty-fifth anniversary, the cable station Comedy Central followed up a marathon of the 1970s serialized sitcom *Soap* with an on-air panel discussion including a number of actors from *All My Children*, who explained how their characters would have handled the various plotlines featured on *Soap*. Among the cast members participating in the discussion were Walt Willey (*Jackson Montgomery*), Kelly Ripa (*Hayley Vaughn*), Michael E. Knight (*Tad Martin*), Cady McClain (*Dixie Cooney*), Sydney Penny (*Julia Santos*), Keith Hamilton Cobb (*Noah Keefe*), and Sarah Michelle Gellar (*Kendall Hart*).

1995: No soap opera has celebrated an anniversary with more fanfare than *All My Children* did its twenty-fifth. A week of special episodes brought back more than twenty old cast members and included clips from the show's past. On-screen the characters came back to town for a housewarming party at Joe and Ruth Martin's new home. On January 15, 1995, Carol Burnett hosted a prime-time special in which she interviewed cast members, past and present, and introduced clips. A best-selling coffee table book, *All My Children: The Complete Family Scrapbook*, by Gary Warner, was also published to mark the occasion.

1995: While the O. J. Simpson trial preempted soaps off and on during 1994 and 1995, Kimberly Hawthorne made good use of it. She studied prosecutor Marcia Clark's courtroom mannerisms and demeanor to prepare for her courtroom scenes as lawyer Belinda Keefer.

1995: Because of the bombing of the Federal Building in Oklahoma City, *All My Children* reworked a story line in which Janet Green planned to detonate a bomb at Trevor Dillon's wedding to Laurel Banning. Some of the scenes of Janet building the bomb had already been taped and could not be edited out, so the producers ended those episodes with a message from Robin Mattson, who plays Janet, addressing the difference between fact and fiction.

1995: Marcy Walker (*Liza Colby*) returned to the show after an absence of eleven years. A few months later, Karen Lynn Gorney, who originated the role of Tara Martin, re-

Noah and Julia's wedding (pictured: Eileen Herlie, Michael Nader, Susan Lucci, Socorro Santiago, Raul Davila, Keith Hamilton Cobb, Sydney Penny, Darlene Dahl, and Catherine Gardner). 1996/Ann Limongello

prised it for a six-week stint after an absence of seventeen years.

1996: While daytime has featured a number of interracial relationships and even interracial marriages over the years, the wedding of Noah Keefer and Julia Santos marked the first time that daytime audiences saw a black man marry a white woman. Up till that point, the few interracial weddings soap fans saw involved black women and white men.

1996: *All My Children* became the first soap opera to begin each day with a recap of the previous day's episode and to end with a teaser of the coming day's show. After a few months, *One Life to Live* and *General Hospital* followed suit.

1996: Because of a severe blizzard that hit New York in 1996, very few of the actors were able to make it to the ABC studios. The producers decided that they would tape scenes with whatever actors made it in. T. C. Warner (*Kelsey Jefferson*), who lived nearby, was able to tape her entire week's worth of episodes in one day.

1997: On January 27, *All My Children* taped its seven thousandth episode.

Backstage Pass

Phoebe Tyler Wallingford, as played by Ruth Warrick, has become one of daytime's most memorable and popular characters. Warrick, however, came close to being fired during her first six months on the show. Because of her own involvement in the civil rights movement and the varied peace marches being held during the early '70s, Warrick had a hard time connecting to Phoebe's distaste for social improvement. As such, she tended to play Phoebe a bit on the foolish side. The director took her out to a restaurant one night and at the end of dinner revealed the purpose of their meeting. If she didn't stop playing Phoebe for laughs, he warned, the producers were going to fire her. "Well, you're a director," she responded. "For heaven's sake, direct me." The director advised Warrick to make Phoebe the sort of woman people feared. Warrick followed his suggestion, which only made the character even more comic and more beloved by the audience.

Rosemary Prinz, who had agreed to play *All My Children*'s Amy Tyler only for the show's first six months,

The triangle of Phoebe, Charles, and Mona (Ruth Warrick, Hugh Franklin, and Frances Heflin). 1979/ABC

recognized Susan Lucci's talent right away. Before leaving, Prinz advised Lucci, "Don't get stuck here." Years later, after establishing herself as daytime's leading lady, Lucci ran into Prinz at a function and reminded Prinz of the advice she'd given years before. Prinz couldn't help but laugh.

As Joe Martin was comforting his daughter Tara following a nightmare, Ray MacDonnell leaned in to give Karen Lynn Gorney a hug. When Gorney pulled back, she noticed that during their hug one of her false eyelashes had come off on his cheek. Since the cheek was not visible to the camera, Gorney did not interrupt the taping. She played out the remainder of the scene, trying very hard to ignore the lash fluttering on MacDonnell's cheek every time he spoke.

Once, while getting ready to tape a scene, Lucci decided that she wanted to wear a hat she had worn before.

The costume room was empty, and the lights were low when she got there. In a rush to get back to the set, Lucci didn't notice that the trapdoor to the storage room had been left open. She fell eight feet down to the basement below. After being rescued, she grabbed the hat she was looking for and headed back to tape the scene.

Frances Heflin (*Mona Kane*) forgot to wear her contact lenses during a scene in which Mona was hemming a skirt that Erica was wearing. Unable to see what she was doing, Heflin sewed the skirt to her own dress, a mistake that became apparent as soon as Erica started to walk away from Mona.

Even though Eileen Herlie (*Myrtle Fargate*) was auditioning for the role of a homeless ex–carnival worker, she dressed up as nicely as she could when she went to meet with the producers the first time. Her first day on the set, wardrobe outfitted her with an ugly polka dot-dress, a ragged brown cardigan, a red wig, and a white beret. Herlie did her own makeup, laying it on extra thick. The transformation was so convincing that director Henry Kaplan, whom she met during her first visit to the show, did not recognize her. He stopped her in the hallway to let her know that uninvited guests were not welcome in the studio.

Peter White wasn't quite sure what to make of Ruth Warrick the first time that he did a scene with her after taking over the role of Phoebe's son Lincoln. During their very first scene together, Warrick unbuttoned his shirt and removed the belt from around his waist. Unwilling to say anything because of Warrick's status as the star, White continued with his lines as best he could. It wasn't until he'd gotten all the way through the scene and heard the crew laughing that he realized it was all a joke.

Charles Frank (*Jeff Martin*) enjoyed trying to distract

his on-screen stepmother Mary Fickett (*Ruth Martin*). He would often hide underneath the nurses' station and wait until the time came for her close-up. While she delivered her dialogue, he would run his hands up and down her legs.

Francesca James (*Kitty Shea*) played a joke on her cast mates during her on-screen funeral. With the help of her leading man Peter White (*Lincoln Tyler*) and Robin Strasser (*Dr. Christine Karras*), James snuck into Kitty's coffin just before the cast and crew arrived. As soon as everyone was in place, James knocked on the coffin lid and surprised everyone with an impromptu resurrection.

After James returned to the show as Kitty's twin sister Kelly, one fan wrote to the producers asking why, if they had to introduce Kitty's twin sister, couldn't they have found an actress who at least looked like Kitty.

Roscoe Orman was balancing a recurring role as Donna Beck's (Candice Earley) pimp Tyrone with a regular part on the children's series *Sesame Street*. After a while, he learned that some of the children who knew him as Gordon on *Sesame Street* were also seeing him rough up women as Tyrone on *All My Children*. For the sake of his *Sesame Street* fans, Orman opted to leave *All My Children*.

Juggling his work on *All My Children* with a play he was doing at night took its toll on Larry Keith (*Nick Davis*). He fell asleep during the taping of a scene one day. Nick was sitting down while Frances Heflin delivered a speech as Mona. Keith took advantage of Mona's two-page monologue and the fact that the camera was on her to steal forty winks. Just before Heflin finished her speech, she kicked the bottom of Keith's foot so that he would be awake when the camera cut back to him. To his credit, Keith jumped right into the scene where he belonged—

which did not save him from a second, unscripted lecture from Heflin.

Susan Plantt Wilson discovered that her character Claudette Montgomery was being killed off after she overheard the prop men discussing Claudette's upcoming car crash.

For some reason, Mark LaMura (*Mark Dalton*) had a mental block against remembering the simple line ''I love you'' during the scenes with his longtime leading lady Kathleen Noone (*Ellen Shepherd Dalton*). Noone, who has large eyes, poked a little fun at LaMura by writing the words ''I love you'' on her eyelids. When he faltered during taping one day, Noone simply shut her eyes.

One scene called for Palmer Cortandt (James Mitchell) to lash out at a painting of his presumedly dead wife Daisy (Gillian Spencer) with a fireplace poker. Mitchell got a little carried away. The poker got caught in the set and knocked it down.

At the same time that Gil Rogers was playing Tad Martin's villainous father Ray Gardner on *All My Children*, he could be seen during the commercial breaks as a kindly grandfather, teaching his grandson the wonders of nature and Grape Nuts cereal. The company worried about the soap fans associating one of its spokespersons with crimes like rape and attempted murder. Ray Gardner was soon killed off.

When the show was picking out a wedding band for Dottie Thornton's (Tasia Valenza) wedding to Tad Martin (Michael E. Knight), Valenza took off an old ring for the costume designer to measure. She didn't take into consideration the fact that the ring was old and that she had been forcing it on for years. So when the time came for Tad to place the ring upon her finger during the wedding ceremony, Knight couldn't get it past her knuckle.

Cady McClain (*Dixie Cooney*) did not get her driver's license until she learned that she needed to have one for a scene in which Dixie accidentally hits Billy Clyde Tuggle with her car. She took a crash course that sent her onto the hazardous streets of New York City. The amount of driving she did on the show totaled only about 150 feet. After that a stunt driver took over for her.

Larkin Malloy also had to take driving lessons for the scene in which Travis Montgomery competed in an auto race.

Teresa Blake (*Gloria Marsh*) was a little intimidated when she learned that her storyline would have her working extensively with David Canary (*Adam* and *Stuart Chandler*). Cady McClain, who had worked with Canary since her first day on the job, took Blake aside and assured her that in real life, Canary was "more Stuart than Adam."

Walt Willey (*Jackson Montgomery*) had a little trouble concentrating during his first scene with David Canary—but not because he was intimidated. The minute Willey saw Canary, the theme from Canary's prime-time series *Bonanza* started playing in Willey's mind and continued playing throughout that whole first scene.

Sydney Penny's (*Julia Santos*) fear of needles made it especially difficult for her to do the scene in which Julia takes an AIDS test after being raped. Even though a fake syringe filled with phony blood was used for the scene, Penny couldn't look at it. She couldn't even watch the extra playing the nurse tie the rubber hose around her arm.

Carter Jones's reign of terror in Pine Valley left two of John Wesley Shipp's co-stars a little worse for wear. Because Jessica Collins's character, Dinah Lee Mayberry, wore tight clothes, the wardrobe people couldn't outfit her with any padding the way they did with James Kiberd (*Tre-*

vor Dillon), Jean LeClerc (*Jeremy Hunter*), and Shipp himself. The fight scene between Carter and Dinah left Collins with more than a couple of bruises on her knees. Later, while rehearsing a scene in which Carter was struggling with Natalie Dillon, Melody Anderson tripped and took an unscripted fall down a flight of stairs. In doing so, she picked up a couple of scrapes and minor cuts. Rather than hold up taping with a trip to the hospital, Anderson finished the scene after being checked out by a paramedic.

Darlene Dahl had never done a kissing scene before the one in which Anita Santos and Bobby Warner go parking. She tried to compensate for her nervousness by coming on too strong. During the rehearsal, Dahl all but threw herself at Brian Gaskill. The producer dropped Dahl a note reminding her that Bobby was the aggressive one in the relationship.

Not all of *All My Children*'s most popular couples have gotten along perfectly together behind the scenes. Both Cady McClain and Michael E. Knight now laugh about the shouting matches the two of them used to get into during their first go-round as Tad and Dixie. The relationship between them improved considerably after Tad came back to the show in the early '90s.

Matt Borlenghi, who played one of Dixie's leading men, Brian Bodine, enjoyed working with McClain but admitted that he and Kelly Ripa (*Hayley Vaughn*), who were quite popular as the show's teen couple, had many a backstage argument.

While in New York for the Daytime Emmys, Peter Bergman (*Cliff Warner*) and his wife passed by the corner of 67th Street and Columbus Avenue, where *All My Children* used to be taped. The building that housed the studio had by that time been leveled, a fact that hit Bergman harder emotionally than he had expected. When Bergman returned to his hotel room later that day, he discovered that his wife had returned to the lot where the studio used to be and took one of the bricks that were lying on the ground. Bergman keeps that brick in his dressing room at *The Young and the Restless.*

Inside Jokes

One of the more interesting legends in *All My Children* history has been that of Bobby Martin (Mike Bersell), Joe Martin's (Ray MacDonnell) son who went up to polish his skis one night and was never seen or spoken of again. There is a kernel of truth to the Bobby Martin story; Joe Martin did have a son Bobby, but the character was forgotten about at summer camp, not in his room polishing skis. Some twenty years after Bobby's mysterious disappearance, the writers decided to finally address the issue of Bobby, if only in jest. Opal Purdy (Jill Larson), who was staying with the Martins, accidentally locked herself in the attic. While hunting around for something she could use to escape, she came across a skeleton sitting next to a pair of skis. Hanging over the skull was a baseball cap with the name Bobby on it.

Susan Lucci has poked fun at her Emmy losing streak on *Saturday Night Live*, in the commercial for the sugar substitute the Sweet One and on *All My Children* itself. In one story line, Edmund Grey (John Callahan) kidnaped

Erica Kane (Susan Lucci) during her romantic vacation with Dimitri Marrick (Michael Nader) in Budapest. After getting the impression that Dimitri had reconciled with his wife Angelique (Season Hubley), Erica teamed up with Edmund to continue the charade of being kidnapped. During a phone conversation with Dimitri, Erica carried on as though she were being tortured by Edmund. When she hung up, Edmund applauded her performance. "You deserve an Oscar," he told her. Erica quickly shot back, "I'd settle for an Emmy."

During a conversation about women, Jake Martin (Michael Lowry) told his mother Ruth (Lee Meriwether), "I've never seen a Miss America as pretty as my mom." The compliment was an obvious reference to the fact that the role of Ruth Martin was now being played by Meriwether, a former Miss America.

After Trevor Dillon (James Kiberd) invited Janet Green (Robin Mattson) to dinner, she expressed some concern over his culinary talents. "Trust Chef Dillon," he assured her. "I watch *The Main Ingredient*." It was a sly reference to the cooking show that Mattson hosts on the Lifetime channel.

When Adam Chandler (David Canary) blackmailed Erica Kane into a "remarriage," she expressed her true feelings about their union by wearing a black dress to the wedding. While the visual image of Erica in the black wedding dress worked as a joke on the show, it was probably not a coincidence that Susan Lucci had recently starred in a highly rated TV movie titled *The Bride in Black*.

Marcy Walker's two-year stint on the CBS soap *Guiding Light* has been mined for a couple of inside jokes. During the show's twenty-fifth-anniversary week, Tad Martin (Michael E. Knight) wondered aloud to brother Joey

(Michael Brainard) what Liza Colby was up to. Joey mentioned that he heard she was living in Springfield—where *Guiding Light* is set.

After Walker returned to the show and Liza took over the job of station manager at WRCW, Tad once introduced her as a producer, general manager, and "overall guiding light." Liza responded, "Guiding light? I don't think so." It had been general knowledge in the soap opera press that Walker was never thrilled with the way her role worked out on *Guiding Light*.

Over on *All My Children*'s sister soap, *Loving*, modeling agent Tess Wilder (Catherine Hickland) hung up the telephone after a conversation with Tad Martin (*Michael E. Knight*). Tess, who had met him offscreen at one point, mentioned what a cute guy he was. In real life, Hickland is married to Knight.

Frances Heflin, who played Erica Kane's mother Mona, had been given a cameo in the film *Mr. Billions*, directed by her real-life son Jonathan Kaplan. In one scene, Heflin's character picks up the phone and says, "Hello, Erica. How are you, honey?"

Con artist Wade Matthews (Christopher Holder) was one time pumping Edna Thornton (Sandy Gabriel) for information about the various people who lived in Pine Valley. After a couple of minutes summarizing the residents' sordid histories and connections with one another, Edna remarked that she sometimes felt as if she were living in "one of those soap operas that my daughter watches."

The Thin Line Between Fiction and Reality

When Eileen Letchworth, who played Margo Flax, was contemplating a face-lift, she talked it over with Agnes Nixon. Not only was Letchworth going to need time off, she was going to look significantly different when she returned to the show. Nixon approved and actually worked the face-lift into Margo's story line. Margo wanted to impress the somewhat younger Paul Martin (William Mooney). With Letchworth's face-lift incorporated into Margo's story line, Letchworth did not need to take as much time off. She and her alter ego Margo recovered from their face-lift on-screen.

Brooke English's (Julia Barr) story lines have often been wrapped up in the plight of the homeless. She discovered that her biological mother was living among them; she opened up The Brooke English House, helping the homeless; and most recently, she adopted Laura Kirk (Lauren Roman), who had been living on the streets since her mother died. Barr herself has been equally commit-

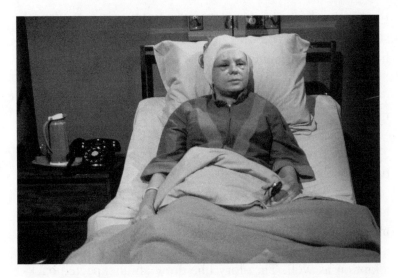

Eileen Letchworth (*Margo Flax*) recovered from a real-life face-lift on camera. 1974/Ann Limongello

ted to helping the homeless. She has been the celebrity spokesperson for The Company of Women, a national merchandise catalog whose proceeds help to fund the New York–based Rockland Family Shelter helping battered women and children, rape victims, and the homeless. Barr has also used her celebrity status to help The Coalition for the Homeless and its First Step program in preparing homeless women to join the workforce. Just as Brooke was honored in 1995 for her efforts to help the homeless, the following year Barr was similarly honored.

Like Julia Barr, Susan Lucci has also followed in the footsteps of her on-screen persona, Erica Kane. Erica Kane started her own cosmetics line in the late '80s. While she wanted to name the company after herself, the Montgomery brothers, her investors, convinced her to call the company

Enchantment. Susan Lucci has been able to go Erica one step better. Lucci is CEO of a line of hair care products bearing her own name, The Susan Lucci Collection.

Fred Porcelli managed to balance his role as a maître d' named Freddy at the Chateau with his nighttime job as maître d' at New York's prestigious "21" Club.

Richard Shoberg headed down to Saint Croix to film Tom and Erica's honeymoon a mere two weeks after getting married himself.

After Lisa Wilkinson (*Nancy Grant*) and her real-life husband John Danelle, who played Nancy's on-screen husband Frank, mentioned that they were considering adopting a child, their onscreen counterparts began talking about adoption as well. The story line drew an unexpected backlash from a number of viewers who saw Frank and Nancy's decision to adopt as a sort of genocide. An unplanned pregnancy was written into Nancy's story line, and talk of adoption quickly ended. Shortly after learning that Nancy was pregnant, Wilkinson discovered she herself was pregnant as well. Wilkinson's own unplanned and coincidental pregnancy prompted her husband Danelle to jokingly dub head writer Agnes Nixon "the Witch of Television."

Patricia Barry had been trying to land an acting role in New York City so that she could help her daughter prepare for her upcoming wedding. After moving to California to look for work, she was able to return to New York when *All My Children* hired her as Brooke English's mother Peg. Just like Barry herself, Peg English arrived in Pine Valley to help Brooke plan her upcoming wedding to Tom Cudahy.

Candice Earley, who had played reformed teen prostitute Donna Beck Tyler, was detained outside the studio one night by a police officer who was sure that Earley herself was a hooker the police had been looking for. Earley tried to convince the officer that he probably recognized her from the show. Although he didn't admit it, he did let her go.

Larkin Malloy liked the way that his character Travis Montgomery's office was furnished so much that he went out and bought the exact same furniture to decorate the office in his own apartment.

Michael Lowry, the son of a doctor, dropped out of medical school to pursue a career in acting. One of his first story lines as Jake Martin was explaining to his father, Dr. Joe Martin, that he had left medical school. Like Lowry, he moved into show business, working the cameras at WRCW. Unlike Lowry, though, Jake has returned to medicine.

From Headlines to Plotlines

All My Children has long been heralded as one of the most socially progressive soap operas on television, dealing with important issues, ranging from medicine to politics. Creator Agnes Nixon had written one of daytime's first social issue stories back in the early '60s—Bert Bauer's battle with uterine cancer on *Guiding Light*. Nixon also launched the socially relevant *One Life to Live* in 1968. Throughout the years, Nixon has had a knack for figuring out which news stories would make good soap opera stories and then connecting them with the right characters.

All My Children debuted during the Vietnam War, a fact that was not ignored by Nixon. Among her very first story lines, Amy Tyler's (Rosemary Prinz) involvement in the peace movement put her at odds with her mother-in-law Phoebe Tyler (Ruth Warrick). The war was allowed to play an even more prominent role two years later when Richard Hatch, who played Amy's biological son Phil Brent, wanted to leave the show. In one of the most dramatic departures ever written for a soap character, Phil Brent was drafted and presumed missing in action. With Rosemary Prinz already off the show, Phil's biological mother Ruth Martin (Mary Fickett) took over Amy's role on the show as antiwar advocate and won an Emmy for her role.

In the landmark 1973 case *Roe* v. *Wade*, the Supreme Court legalized abortion. The first television series on either daytime or prime-time to dramatize a legal abortion was *All My Children*. (Approximately ten years prior, *Another World*'s young heroine Pat Matthews had undergone an illegal abortion.) Erica Kane (Susan Lucci) worried that her pregnancy would bring an end to her modeling career. Although the Supreme Court ruled that abortion was a woman's choice, the story line highlighted another aspect of the situation: doctors would not perform an abortion without a husband's consent. So, Erica said she was single, since she had no intention of telling her husband, Jeff Martin (Charles Frank), that she was pregnant. Jeff found out the truth after Erica was hospitalized with an infection that was a direct result of the abortion. Although abortion was legal, Nixon realized that many people in the audience did not approve of it. When Erica's mother Mona (Frances Heflin) asked Jeff to forgive Erica, she was in a sense asking the audience to forgive Erica as well.

Nixon tackled the abortion question a number of times over the years, most recently with the character of Julia Santos (Sydney Penny). After Julia was raped, she discovered that she was pregnant. Rather than give birth to her rapist's child, Julia opted to have an abortion. Her decision came at a time when abortion clinics were being targeted for violence by radical pro-life organizations. As Julia made her way into the clinic, Tom Cudahy (Richard Shoberg) held his sign with a pro-life group outside the clinic as a model on how to conduct a peaceful demonstration.

The character of Donna Beck (Francesca Poston, later Candice Earley), the teen prostitute with whom Chuck Tyler (Richard Van Vleet) falls in love, was conceived after Agnes Nixon read a newspaper article titled "Little Ladies of the Night," detailing the plight of runaways from the Midwest who had become prostitutes in New York City.

When Susan Blanchard (*Mary Kennicott Martin*) and Charles Frank (*Jeff Martin*) decided to leave *All My Children* in 1975, Agnes Nixon decided that the best way to handle the situation would be for Mary to be killed off. After reading Stewart Alsop's book *Stay of Execution*, Nixon had been considering a leukemia story line for Mary in which she is ultimately cured of the disease. Shortly before Blanchard made her decision to leave, Nixon began dropping hints to the effect that Mary was sick. While the pieces were in place for Nixon to have Mary die from leukemia, that was not the story Nixon wanted to tell. She wanted to relay a story with hope, not one that would scare viewers. Nixon was also less than thrilled with the idea of a fatal car crash, since the budget at the time would not allow the crash to be seen. She stumbled upon the perfect way for Mary to die in a Philadelphia newspaper. A father and son had been traveling up and down the East Coast, tricking their way into homes, only to then rob and kill the owners. Nixon could envision the somewhat naive Mary Kennicott Martin letting strangers into her home if they appeared to be in need. An element of heroism befitting the character was added to Mary's murder. A young Tad Martin (Matthew Anton), whom Mary and Jeff were planning to adopt, came by for a visit. Rather than let him become another hostage, Mary warned him to run away. One of the gunmen in turn shot Mary dead.

During the late '70s and early '80s, story lines were harvested from some amazing breakthroughs that were being made in the world of medicine. Ruth Martin's joy over being pregnant with Joe's child was tempered with the fear that women over forty, as she was, faced greater risks of giving birth to children with severe health problems. Ruth considered an abortion but underwent an amniocentesis, which in 1979 was just becoming common practice. Many viewers heard about it for the first time on *All My Children*. When the amniocentesis procedure assured Ruth that her child carried none of the illnesses she was worried about, she saw the pregnancy all the way through.

A year later, Nina Cortlandt (Taylor Miller) began losing her eyesight because of diabetic retinopathy. Her impending blindness was manipulated by her father Palmer (James Mitchell) to keep her away from Cliff Warner (Peter Bergman). Before beginning this story line, Nixon knew that Nina's vision could be saved through laser surgery. The story line took Miller and *All My Children* on location to the Wilmer Ophthalmological Institute in Baltimore.

The one medical situation Nixon could not dramatize with a happy ending was the AIDS epidemic. By the late '80s, the epidemic had become such a national crisis, with AIDS-related stories hitting the news on a nightly basis, that the show could not ignore its existence. In 1987, *All My Children* became one of the first soap operas to introduce a front-burner character who was HIV-positive. Cindy Parker (Ellen Wheeler) had contracted the virus from her late husband, a drug addict. Although Mark Dalton (Mark LaMura) had shared needles with Cindy's late husband during his own battle with drugs, he tested negative. While

Stuart Chandler (David Canary) fell for AIDS patient Cindy Parker (Ellen Wheeler). 1988/Ann Limongello

Nixon couldn't give Cindy a happy ending, she did teach the audience a lesson about death with dignity and tolerance toward those afflicted with AIDS.

In 1989, Abe and Mary Ayala made national news when they conceived a child to be a bone marrow donor for their teenage daughter Anissa, who suffered from leukemia. *All My Children*'s Travis and Barbara Montgomery (Larkin Malloy and Susan Pratt) also resorted to extreme measures in an attempt to cure their own leukemia-stricken daughter, Molly. Unlike the real-life Ayalas, however, Travis and Barbara were divorced and married to other people at the time: Travis to Erica, and Barbara to Tom. Barbara's pregnancy was used to break up both couples. Luckily, both the real-life and fictional stories ended happily with the newborn child matching the blood type and supplying the much-needed bone marrow for their older sisters.

The famed case of Gregory K., the teenager who "divorced" his negligent parents to live with a more caring foster family, was the inspiration for a similar custody battle on *All My Children*. Jamal Wilson (Amir Jamal Williams), who lost his mother to AIDS, had been taken in by Tom Cudahy and his new wife Livia Frye (Tonya Pinkins). When corporate climber Alec McIntyre (Grant Aleksander) discovered that Jamal was his biological son, he sued for and was awarded custody of the boy. Jamal, in turn, sued Alec to be returned to the couple he had come to accept as his mother and father. Alec ultimately relented and allowed Jamal to live with Tom and Livia.

When Lorraine Broderick took over the head writing chores at *All My Children*, the character of gay high school teacher Michael Delaney (Chris Bruno) was already in place, although his sexuality had not yet been revealed to his students or to the audience. In doing the research on gay teachers, the writing staff came across the case of Rodney Wilson, who like Michael was a history teacher. Wilson had come out to his class during a lecture on the Holocaust. He pointed to a pink triangle and said, "If I had been in Europe during World War Two, I could have been forced to wear this and could have been murdered because I'm gay." Michael Delaney came out to his class in the exact same manner. While some parents complained and some students wrote the word "fag" on his chalkboard, Wilson did not need to sue to keep from losing his job as Michael did. Wilson's mother, a fan of the show, saw the classroom coming-out scene and immediately called up her son to tell him about it.

Crossovers

In 1979, when *One Life to Live*'s Viki Buchanan (Erika Slezak) went on trial for the murder of Marco Dane (Gerald Anthony), Paul Martin (William Mooney) traveled from Pine Valley to nearby Llanview to defend her. Five years later, when Viki's husband Clint Buchanan (Clint Ritchie) went on trial for the murder of Echo di Savoy (Kim Zimmer), Viki hired Paul Martin as his lawyer. By this time, it should be noted, Mooney had already left *All My Children*.

When Adam Chandler (David Canary) fired Liza Colby (Marcy Walker) from her job as station manager at WRCW after she slept with Tad Martin (Michael E. Knight), Liza hired *One Life to Live*'s legal eagle Nora Buchanan (Hillary B. Smith) to represent her in a sexual harassment case. One conversation between Adam and Nora was all it took for Liza to get her job back.

Adam Chandler, in one of his many efforts to make life hell for his wife Natalie (Kate Collins), got in touch with *One Life to Live*'s Dorian Lord (then played by Elaine Princi), who was publishing the tabloid *The National In-*

truder at the time. Princi was seen in a phone conversation with Adam, in which he fed Dorian embarrassing information about his wife.

Tad Martin traveled to Llanview to do a show on country clubs and ran into fellow reporter Kevin Buchanan (Kevin Stapleton). A couple of weeks later, Kevin, along with his ex-girlfriend Rachel Gannon (Sandra P. Grant) and her family, traveled to Pine Valley to discuss Rachel's drug addiction on Tad's talk show, *The Cutting Edge*. Although the scene took place in Pine Valley, it aired on *One Life to Live*. Michael E. Knight, Teresa Blake (*Gloria Marsh*), and the *Cutting Edge* set all made the trip over to the *One Life to Live* studios.

In 1993, ABC tried to boost the ratings for *Loving* by sending to Corinth one of its more popular Pine Valley couples, Jeremy Hunter (Jean LeClerc) and Ceara Connor (Genie Francis). Jeremy was invited to Corinth by Trisha Alden (played by Noelle Beck), who came to *All My Children* for a day. Ceara took a public relations–fund-raising job at Alden University. Although Jeremy and Ceara were on the outs, their time in Corinth helped them mend fences and get back together. Eventually, Jeremy was shipped over to Corinth on a permanent basis. The character of Ceara was shipped off to England and then killed off. On his way to Corinth, Jeremy also stopped by *One Life to Live*, where he rescued some of Viki Buchanan's paintings from a fire. As *Loving* was in the process of being revamped into *The City*, Jeremy was killed by his ex-lover Gwyneth, who'd gone mad and dumped a vat of quick-drying plaster on him, turning the artist into a statue.

Debbi Morgan (*Dr. Angela Hubbard*) left *All My Children* in 1990. She reprised the character of Angie on *Loving* three years later. Eventually Morgan was reunited on *Lov-*

Jeremy Hunter (Jean LeClerc, pictured in left photo with Susan Lucci as Erica Kane and in right photo with Lisa Peluso as Ava Rescott) moved from Pine Valley to *Loving*'s Corinth. 1985/L. Corbett

ing with her most popular leading man, Darnell Williams (who was introduced as a Jessie Hubbard look-alike named Jacob Johnson). At one point, Jacob came face-to-face with Jessie's ghost. Angie's mother Pat Baxter (played by Lee Chamberlain) also turned up on *Loving* from time to time.

Ruth Warrick traveled to *Loving* as Phoebe when she was invited to the party to celebrate Cooper Alden's (Michael Weatherly) engagement to Ally Rescott (Laura Wright).

At one point, *Loving*'s Dinah Lee and Hannah Mayberry (Jessica Collins and Rebecca Gayheart) traveled from Corinth to Pine Valley, where Dinah Lee met up with an old friend, wife beater Carter Allen (John Wesley Shipp). Dinah Lee refused to believe Carter was violent until he took out his aggression on her. Police officer Trevor Dillon

(James Kiberd) and Jeremy Hunter chased Carter to Corinth. Kiberd had originally played Mike Donovan on *Loving* during the 1980s. In one comic scene, Trevor's car collided with that of Mike's ex-lover Shana Vochek (played by Kiberd's real-life wife Susan Keith). The fender bender ended with an argument in which Trevor and Shana insulted each other's spouses.

After *Loving* transformed into *The City*, Walt Willey (*Jackson Montgomery*) visited the show's leading vixen, Sydney Chase (Morgan Fairchild), who turned out to be an ex-lover of his. While the police were investigating the murder of Sydney's husband, Jack offered her free legal advice. In Fairchild's last scene on the show, she convinced Jack to accompany her to London for the weekend.

Despite the fact that characters from *All My Children* traveled from Pine Valley to Corinth and SoHo, characters on both *Loving* and *The City* occasionally referred to *All My Children* as a soap opera. Deborah Brewster (Nancy

Angie and Jessie Hubbard (Debbi Morgan and Darnell Williams) were daytime's first African-American supercouple. 1983/Bob Sacha

Addison Altman) once considered becoming a model "like Erica Kane on *All My Children.*" Aspiring actress Molly Malone went out to audition for roles on *One Life to Live* and *All My Children.*

All the World's a Studio

Although Pine Valley is located in Pennsylvania, the outside scenes of the town were, for the most part, filmed in Connecticut. Cortlandt Manor, for example, is the Waveny Mansion in New Canaan. And when Jeff Martin (Charles Frank) visited his wife Mary's grave for the last time, the scene was filmed in a small Connecticut cemetery. The exterior shots of Pine Valley University were filmed, however, on the campus of Princeton University in New Jersey. The show has also taken advantage of the New York setting outside its doors for some memorable shoots: Cliff and Nina's Central Park wedding, Erica's photo shoot around town, and Noah and Julia's night on the town. On more than one occasion, the producers have taken their cameras not only outside but halfway around the world.

In 1978, *All My Children* became the first soap opera to take its cameras outside the United States. The decision was made to follow Tom and Erica (Richard Shoberg and Susan Lucci) on their honeymoon to the island of Saint Croix. Saint Croix was an appropriate choice, since it was

An avalanche trapped Chuck and Donna (Richard Van Vleet and Candice Earley) in the Swiss Alps. 1982/Steve Fenn

there that Agnes Nixon had originally finished the bible for *All My Children* some thirteen years prior. Among the varied scenes scheduled to take advantage of the island's setting were some of the couple scuba diving. Lucci, who had never gone scuba diving before, asked for a couple of lessons. The night before the scene was to be taped, Shoberg and the camera crew members who were to dive with her gave Lucci an hour of training in the deep end of the pool of the hotel where they were staying. A quick study, Lucci learned enough from that hour in the pool to spend eight hours in the ocean the following day.

All My Children traveled all the way to Switzerland for the scene in which Chuck Tyler (Richard Van Vleet) and Donna Cortlandt (Candice Earley) rediscovered their love. Chuck and Donna were on a skiing trip with their respective new partners and became trapped in a cave overnight.

Reporter Brooke English (Julia Barr) went to prison rather than reveal a source. 1985/Ann Limongello

During this time they made love and conceived a child. Although the snowstorm that trapped Donna and Chuck in the cave was essential to the story line, Europe was experiencing an unseasonal heat wave when the cast and crew arrived. Man-made snow and plastic icicles had to compensate for a lack of the real thing.

In 1985, Brooke English (Julia Barr) was sent to prison for refusing to reveal a source. In order to give the social issue story line added weight, the producers decided to film Brooke's prison scenes on location. Filling in for Statesville Prison, where Brooke was sent, was the famous prison Sing Sing in upstate New York. *All My Children* has remained the only soap opera allowed to film inside the prison.

All My Children traveled to Maine to film the story line in which Trevor Dillon and Natalie Hunter became shipwrecked together. While the characters were fighting with each other through most of the shoot, the actors themselves were battling swarms of mosquitoes that plagued them day and night. Collins and Kiberd had to be covered with bug spray from head to toe before shooting the scene in which Natalie and Trevor finally give in to their mutual attraction on the beach.

One of *All My Children*'s more ambitious and eye-catching location shoots took Erica Kane and Dimitri Marrick (Michael Nader) to Budapest, in his homeland, Hungary. In addition to highlighting the romance between Erica and Dimitri, the remote location had Erica kidnapped twice: once by Dimitri's half-brother Edmund Grey (John Callahan) and another time by Dimitri's mother-in-law Helga (Susan Willis).

The location shoot involved a couple of tricky transportation scenes. Callahan had to learn how to ride a motorcycle for the scene in which Edmund stalks Erica and Dimitri. To compensate for Callahan's inexperience, the scenes in which he is seen riding the motorcycle were kept to a minimum. The cobblestone streets of Budapest also made the car scenes involving Erica and Dimitri especially bumpy. The producers made for a smoother ride by placing Dimitri's car on top of a flatbed truck.

All My Children took its cameras north to the Canadian wilderness for the story line in which Tad's look-alike Ted Orsini (Michael E. Knight) plots to do in Tad and claim his life. In an interesting gender twist on the shining knight and the damsel in distress, Dixie (Cady McClain) realizes that Tad is in trouble and heads to Canada to rescue him. McClain had a little trouble taping the scene in which Dixie rescued Tad from drowning in the Canadian wilderness. McClain had almost drowned as a child and understandably remained afraid of water. When the time came for Dixie to dive into the river to pull Tad to safety, McClain summoned up the courage to do the scene.

In 1996, Noah Keefer (Keith Hamilton Cobb) escaped to Jamaica with his girlfriend Julia Santos (Sydney Penny) to avoid a murder rap. The island provided a backdrop for a voodoo story line in which Noah and Julia faked their own deaths in order to trick Taylor Cannon (Kelli Taylor) into confessing that Noah had killed drug dealer–rapist Louie Greco (Jack Millard) in self-defense. The Speedo bathing suit Cobb was given to wear didn't leave much room for the show to hide a body microphone during the beach scenes. One of the creative behind-the-scenes technicians took advantage of Cobb's trademark dreadlocks to hide the microphone in his hair.

Erica Lucci

After twenty-seven years, playing Erica has become second nature to Lucci, but the women are distinctly different. The following quiz is designed to see if *All My Children* fans know Susan Lucci as well as they do Erica Kane. (Answers on page 199.)

1. Erica Kane's father Eric rose to prominence as what?
   (a) photojournalist
   (b) film director
   (c) novelist
   (d) symphony conductor

2. In what state did Susan Lucci grow up?
   (a) Alaska
   (b) New York

Erica Kane (Susan Lucci) and her mother Mona (Frances Heflin). 1973/ Owen Franken

    (c) California
    (d) Florida

3. What did Erica name her disco?
    (a) Hollywood East
    (b) Panache
    (c) Erica's
    (d) The Steam Pit

4. How many times has Susan Lucci been married in real life?
    (a) once
    (b) twice

(c) three times
(d) never

5. What did Erica Kane title her 1983 autobiography?
   (a) *The Face in the Mirror*
   (b) *A Model Life*
   (c) *Kane and Able*
   (d) *Raising Kane*

6. On what prime-time soap opera did Lucci play an international terrorist?
   (a) *Dallas*
   (b) *Dynasty*
   (c) *Falcon Crest*
   (d) *Melrose Place*

7. In one of her most famous scenes, what type of wild animal did Erica stare down?
   (a) gorilla
   (b) grizzly bear
   (c) lion
   (d) wolf

8. What are the names of Susan Lucci's children?
   (a) Bianca and Ross
   (b) Ceara and Matthew
   (c) Liza and Andreas
   (d) Susan Lucci has no children in real life.

Why did Erica Kane (Susan Lucci) disguise herself as a nun? 1983/Gary Miller

9. What was the name of the campaign in which Erica became the signature model for Sensuelle Cosmetics?
   (a) An American Beauty
   (b) An American Venus
   (c) The Modern Cleopatra
   (d) The Woman of Mystery

10. For which of the following has Susan Lucci not filmed a commercial?
   (a) Ford Motors
   (b) Sunsweet Pitted Prunes
   (c) Wendy's
   (d) The Sweet One

11. What name did Erica use while hiding out from
    Travis Montgomery and waitressing at Al Darby's
    diner?
    (a) Annie
    (b) Lucy
    (c) Rikki
    (d) Sally

12. What popular American standard did Lucci sing on
    the 1983 album *Love in the Afternoon*, featuring
    actors from the ABC soaps?
    (a) "Always"
    (b) "People"
    (c) "Someone to Watch Over Me"
    (d) "I've Got You Under My Skin"

Mrs. Martin Brent Cudahy, Et Cetera, Et Cetera

One of the questions most often asked of the varied soap opera magazines has been: How many times has Erica Kane been married and to whom? It is not an easy question to answer. She has been married ten times, but not all of those unions have been exactly legal. Still, she has racked up an impressive collection of wedding bands. And while Erica does not make the best of wives—as evidenced by her stack of divorce decrees—she certainly has something going for her. Her last three husbands have all walked her down the aisle twice. Her latest, Dimitri Marrick, was prepared to do so for a third time despite the fact that she once tried to kill him.

Husband No. 1: Jeff Martin

At first Erica set her sights on Jeff Martin to unnerve his sister Tara, her high school rival. Becoming Mrs. Jeff Martin, Erica soon realized, would get her out of her mother's house and offer her the status of being a doctor's

wife. Erica soon came to regret her decision. She hated
their small apartment and the long hours Jeff kept at the
hospital. When agent Jason Maxwell hired her as a model,
Erica jumped at the chance and into bed with her boss. That
affair, combined with Erica's previous decision to have an
abortion rather than derail her modeling career with a pregnancy, chipped away at her marriage. Jeff eventually divorced Erica to marry the sympathetic nurse, Mary
Kennicott.

Husband No. 2: Phil Brent

Once again, Erica's long-running feud with Tara Martin
led her into an unhappy marriage. When Phil Brent returned
from Vietnam to find his beloved Tara married to Chuck
Tyler, he turned his attention to Erica Kane, who had
chased him all through high school. Both Erica and Phil
enjoyed Tara's jealous reaction to seeing them together.
What started off as a simple fling took a serious turn when
Erica learned she was pregnant. Although she planned to
have an abortion, Phil talked her into getting married.
Shortly after the wedding, Erica suffered a miscarriage and
a subsequent nervous breakdown. During her time at a san-
itarium, Phil learned that Chuck and Tara's son Charlie was
really his son and that Tara did still love him. He tried to
divorce Erica after her release from the mental hospital, but
she refused to lose him to Tara. Phil's father Nick finally
bribed her into letting his son go with a hostessing job at
the Chateau.

Erica Kane and Tom Cudahy (Susan Lucci and Richard Shoberg) honeymooned in Saint Croix. 1978/Steve Fenn

Husband No. 3: Tom Cudahy

On the rebound from Phil Brent's father Nick, with whom she had an affair, Erica decided that former pro football player Tom Cudahy was the perfect man to make Nick jealous. She also took added pleasure in stealing Tom away from Brooke Cudahy, her new rival in town. Erica enjoyed the status marriage to Tom afforded her, especially the media coverage on them as "a couple to watch out for." Their marriage came to a close when Tom, who always thought

Erica wanted children, discovered the birth control pills she had been taking on the sly. Tom remains the ex-husband with whom Erica has enjoyed the friendliest relationship. The night before her marriage to Adam Chandler, their relationship turned a little more than friendly as they wound up in bed together.

Husband No. 4: Adam Chandler

Multimillionaire Adam Chandler, who was producing the film version of Erica's autobiography, saw her as the ultimate romantic conquest. He lured her into marriage with a starring role in her own biopic. Soon after the wedding, Adam reneged on the deal but kept Erica chained to him with a combination of threats and expensive gifts. Erica finally left Adam for Mike Roy, the writer who had worked with her on the autobiography. What Erica didn't realize for several years was that her divorce from Adam was not legal; his twin brother Stuart had stood in for Adam during the divorce proceedings.

Husband No. 4¼: Mike Roy

During one point where Adam Chandler faked his own death, Erica married Mike Roy. When Adam turned up alive, her marriage to Mike was declared null and void. Mike and she privately exchanged wedding vows and rings on his deathbed a few months after her "divorce" from Adam.

Erica Kane (Susan Lucci) was caught between brothers Travis and Jackson Montgomery (Larkin Malloy and Walt Willey). 1990/Ann Limongello

Husband No. 4½ and No. 4¾: Travis Montgomery

Erica married the wealthy Travis Montgomery twice, neither time legally because, unbeknownst to her, she was still married to Adam Chandler. Travis and she "married" the first time shortly after Erica gave birth to their daughter Bianca. In desperate need of money, Travis faked his own kidnapping. The unscrupulous Steven Andrews, who kidnapped Travis, later took Bianca. After the baby was returned, Erica took Bianca and left Travis. While hiding out, she met Steven (whom she didn't realize was the criminal mastermind behind the kidnappings) and fell into an affair with him. Travis killed Steven in self-defense and divorced Erica. Bianca's life-threatening bout with Reyes syndrome brought them back together. Although Erica had fallen in love with Travis's brother Jack, she remarried Travis for Bianca's sake. Still, she couldn't stay away from Jack.

Travis meanwhile conceived a child with his ex-wife Barbara as a bone marrow donor for their leukemia-stricken daughter Molly. Travis and Erica's second "marriage" ended with a bitter custody battle that cost Erica her daughter and her relationship with Travis's brother Jackson. Erica broke away from Jackson after he refused to lie on the witness stand about their relationship. Erica and Jackson have tried to reconcile a number of times but have yet to sustain a relationship for more than a few weeks.

Husband No. 4 (continued): Adam Chandler

While working together at Enchantment, Adam rediscovered feelings for Erica. He revealed that their divorce was not legal and blackmailed Erica into a "remarriage." Hoping to appeal the custody decision that gave her daughter Bianca to Travis Montgomery, Erica couldn't risk a public scandal, so she gave in to Adam's demands and proceeded to make his life miserable. After a few months, Adam realized that she would never love him and granted her a real divorce.

Husband No. 5 and No. 6: Dimitri Marrick

Erica and the wealthy royal Dimitri Marrick reluctantly fell in love after he raided her cosmetics company Enchantment. Their love-hate relationship has been one of the more fiery in Erica's long history with the opposite sex. Their first marriage was sabotaged before the wedding ceremony by Kendall Hart, a daughter Erica had given up for adoption at birth. When Dimitri agreed to help Kendall discover her biological father, the man who had raped a teenage

Erica, Erica moved out of the house. Kendall fueled their marital problems by lying to Erica, saying that Dimitri had raped her. Erica flipped out and plunged a letter opener into Dimitri's chest, ending their first marriage. Dimitri, however, understood Erica's mental state and eventually forgave the murder attempt. They remarried on New Year's Eve 1994. Their second marriage was destroyed by Erica's addiction to the painkillers she took after falling off a scaffold. When Dimitri caught Erica in bed with the doctor who had been supplying her with drugs, he filed for divorce. Once again, Dimitri forgave Erica and they reconciled. They came close to getting married for a third time when Erica discovered that she was pregnant by Dimitri. A miscarriage interrupted the ceremony, after which Erica learned that Dimitri had slept with his sister-in-law Maria Santos and had presumably impregnated her as well.

The Last Names Erica Didn't Add to Her Own

Not every man that Erica went after ended up at the altar with her. Some she dumped for greener (as in the color of money) pastures. As hard as it is to believe, a few actually turned her down. And a couple of others just wound up dead.

Tyler

When *All My Children* began, Erica Kane was dating fellow student Chuck Tyler, whose grandmother didn't approve of the relationship because the Kanes were socially beneath the Tylers. Erica's mother Mona actually worked for Chuck's grandfather. Chuck didn't care about social status, but he was in love with another young woman, Tara Martin.

Phoebe did not balk so much when Erica pursued her son Lincoln Tyler, even though Erica was still married to Phil Brent at the time. Phoebe actually encouraged the relationship between Erica and Linc. The Kanes were still beneath the Tylers, but Erica was, in Phoebe's mind, several rungs above Lincoln's true love, Kitty Shea. Erica proved to be a passing fancy for Linc, who reunited with Kitty.

Maxwell

Agent Jason Maxwell traded modeling assignments for sexual favors with Erica, who willingly obliged. Although Erica planned to become Jason's wife, her mother, Mona, accidentally killed him during a struggle with a gun, then blocked out the incident.

Davis

Erica never planned to fall in love with her ex-father-in-law Nick Davis. And he certainly never planned to fall for his son Phil's ex-wife. Almost from the beginning of the show, Erica disliked Nick, who was her mother's friend. They discovered feelings for one another when Erica began working for Nick as hostess at the Chateau. Ironically, Nick had given her that job in exchange for her granting his son Phil a divorce. Although the relationship surprised many fans, it made sense for Erica, who had been abandoned by her own father, to try to fill that void with Nick Davis, a close friend of her mother's who often bossed her around. Nick and Erica broke up after Mona caught them in bed together. Nick suspected that Erica had engineered the situation so that Mona would pressure him into marrying her daughter. It was one scheme too many as far as Nick was concerned. Ironically, it was not a scheme.

Years later, Nick Davis congratulated Erica on hitting the trifecta when she became engaged to his grandson,

Charlie Brent. The two became an item after Charlie was hired as the male model for Erica's cosmetics company, making Erica one of the very few soap opera vixens to bed down with men from three generations of the same family.

Dalton

Erica and music teacher Mark Dalton brought their budding romance to a hasty conclusion after discovering that they shared the same father.

Kingsley

Erica fell for another one of her bosses, Brandon Kingsley, the married cosmetics executive who hired her to represent his company as its spokesmodel. Erica soon tired of waiting for Brandon to leave his wife and was wooed away from Brandon by the significantly wealthier—and less attached—Kent Bogard.

Bogard

Kent Bogard began his relationship with Erica as her secret admirer, sending her expensive gifts and monitoring her every move. He even went so far as to buy the cosmetics company where she was working. When Erica realized who her admirer was, she was intrigued. While Erica planned a future as Kent's wife, Kent remained a playboy and fell into an affair with Connie Wilkes, an impostor passing herself off as Erica's sister, Silver Kane. When Erica found out about their affair, she planned to shoot herself but accidentally killed Kent instead when he struggled with her over the gun.

Hunter

Jeremy's vow of celibacy at a Tibetan lamasery made him Erica's greatest challenge to date. Eventually, she did wear him down; he renounced his vow and made love to her. Erica stood by Jeremy as he went to jail twice for murders he didn't commit. During his second incarceration, Erica tried to help him escape. When Jeremy chose to stay and fight his case legally rather than run away with Erica, the spoiled child in Erica broke off their relationship.

The Marrying Kind

While no one in Pine Valley has walked down the aisle as often as Erica Kane, many of her neighbors and a couple of her ex-husbands have racked up their share of frequent flier miles jetting off to the Caribbean for quickie divorces.

Adam Chandler

Already divorced when he hit Pine Valley, Adam has nonetheless proceeded to get married seven more times since his arrival in town. Technically, he only got married three more times. His marriages to Brooke, Dixie, and Natalie didn't count because he was never legally divorced from Erica. For that same reason his second marriage to Erica was really only a continuation of the existing marriage after a very long and complicated separation. Wives: Althea Chandler, Erica Kane, Brooke English (illegal), Dixie Cooney (illegal), Natalie Hunter (illegal), Erica Kane (technically a continuation of their marriage), Gloria Marsh, and Liza Colby.

Tad Martin (Michael E. Knight) married Dixie Cooney (Cady McClain) twice. 1989/Ann Limongello; 1994/Ann Limongello

Palmer Cortlandt

Adam Chandler may have been married more often, but all of Palmer's six weddings have been legal. Wives: Daisy Cortlandt, Donna Beck, Daisy Cortlandt (again), Cynthia Preston, Natalie Hunter, and Opal Gardner Purdy.

Tad Martin

With his charm and wandering eye, Tad Martin is in position to overtake Palmer Cortlandt and Adam Chandler as the most married man in Pine Valley. Barely into his thirties, Tad has already walked down the aisle five times. Wives: Dottie Thornton, Hillary Wilson, Dixie Cooney, Brooke English, and Dixie Cooney (again).

Tom Cudahy

At one point, Tom Cudahy had considered entering the priesthood. Given his track record with the opposite sex, there were probably many times when he wished that he had followed that path. Despite the Catholic church's stance on divorce, Cudahy has exited holy matrimony five times. Wives: Erica Kane, Brooke English, Skye Chandler, Barbara Montgomery, and Livia Frye.

Natalie Hunter

Although Natalie was introduced fifteen years after Erica, she pulled up right behind her former rival in the wedding march. Widowed shortly after her introduction, Natalie went on to marry five more times, more than half of them legally. At this rate, she stood a good chance of surpassing Erica's record—which might have happened if she weren't killed in a car accident, ironically on her way to one of Erica's weddings. Natalie's husbands: Alex Hunter, Jeremy Hunter (illegal—Erica hired a phony minister), Palmer Cortlandt, Jeremy Hunter, Adam Chandler (illegal—he was still married to Erica Kane), and Trevor Dillon.

Dixie Cooney

If Dixie Cooney ever comes back to Pine Valley, she might give Erica Kane a run for her money in the wedding department. During her eight years in town, she got married five times. She would garner more sympathy as the cheated-upon wife if she hadn't been the other woman in two other marriages. Husbands: Adam Chandler (illegal—he was still married to Erica Kane), Tad Martin, Craig Lawson, Brian Bodine, and Tad Martin (again).

The Love Connection

All My Children first won the hearts of soap fans with the romance between Phil Brent and Tara Martin. In addition to some of daytime's best young love stories, the show has featured some great romances between the more mature characters such as Charles Tyler and Mona Kane. The following quiz pays homage to *All My Children*'s greatest love stories. (Answers on page 199.)

1. How were Phil Brent and Tara Martin related?
   (a) Tara became Phil's aunt by marriage.
   (b) They were step-brother and -sister.
   (c) They were distant cousins.
   (d) Tara became Phil's stepmother.

2. Where were Joe and Ruth Martin married?
   (a) in the Martin living room
   (b) in the hospital chapel

Joe Martin (Ray MacDonnell) married Ruth Brent (Mary Fickett) in 1972.
1972/Ken Regan

(c) on a cruise ship
(d) in Phoebe Tyler's garden

3. In what capacity was Mona Kane working for Dr.
Charles Tyler when she fell in love with him?
(a) accountant
(b) nurse

(c) secretary
(d) housekeeper

4. From what medical condition did Kitty Shea die
shortly after marrying Lincoln Tyler?
   (a) weak heart
   (b) brain tumor
   (c) leukemia
   (d) pancreatic cancer

5. How did Dr. Chuck Tyler meet teenage prostitute
Donna Beck, who would twice become his wife?
   (a) She stole his wallet.
   (b) He found her asleep in the backseat of his car.
   (c) She was his first patient.
   (d) She had been hired as a stripper for his
       bachelor party when he married Tara Martin.

6. Dr. Cliff Warner first met his future love, young
heiress Nina Cortlandt, when she was wheeled into the
hospital. For what did Cliff treat Nina?
   (a) appendicitis
   (b) diabetic shock
   (c) alcohol poisoning
   (d) sunstroke

7. With whom did Langley Wallingford cheat on
Phoebe?
   (a) Edna Thornton

Palmer Cortlandt (James Mitchell, seated) schemed to keep his daughter Nina (Taylor Miller) away from Dr. Cliff Warner (Peter Bergman). 1979/ Steve Fenn

(b) Myrtle Fargate
(c) Marion Colby
(d) Opal Gardner

8. What did Mark Dalton's mother Maureen have against his relationship with Ellen Shepherd?
   (a) Ellen was a divorcée.

   (b) Ellen was ten years older than Mark.
   (c) Ellen had once had an affair with Maureen's
       husband.
   (d) Maureen worried that Ellen was interfering in
       Mark's music career.

9. What incident prompted Greg Nelson to break off
his engagement to Jenny Gardner?
   (a) Jenny kissed Tony Barclay.
   (b) Jenny was offered a modeling job in Paris.
   (c) Greg got drunk and slept with Liza Colby.
   (d) Greg was paralyzed and confined to a
       wheelchair.

10. For what crime did Angie and Jesse go on trial
together?
   (a) murder
   (b) attempted murder
   (c) kidnapping
   (d) possession of drugs

11. What nearly killed the guests at Cindy Parker and
Stuart Chandler's wedding?
   (a) a tornado
   (b) a bomb
   (c) a fire
   (d) carbon monoxide

Jenny (Kim Delaney) danced with Greg (Laurence Lau) at their senior prom. 1982/Leslie Wong

12. Why did Charlie Brent and Julie Chandler pretend to be a couple before they actually got together as one?
    (a) Charlie was trying to make Robin McCall jealous.
    (b) Charlie was trying to make Cecily Davidson jealous.
    (c) Julie was trying to make Nico Kelly jealous.
    (d) Someone had spread a rumor that Charlie was gay.

13. Why did Noah and Julia leave town together?
    (a) Julia's family couldn't accept Noah.
    (b) Noah was offered a modeling contract in Europe.

Julia and Noah (Sydney Penny and Keith Hamilton Cobb) won a *Soap Opera Digest* award in 1996 for Hottest Romance. 1996/Donna Svennevik

    (c) Noah was offered a role on a West Coast soap opera.
    (d) They entered the Witness Protection Program.

14. Who was Edmund Grey trying to get over when he started dating Maria Santos?
    (a) Angelique Marrick

(b) Brooke English
(c) Ceara Connor
(d) Dixie Cooney

15. In what less than romantic setting were Hayley and Mateo married?
    (a) in the hospital parking lot
    (b) in Tom Cudahy's gym
    (c) in a cave
    (d) in a hospital room

Have You Met My Mother?

Nothing intensifies a love triangle more than making the two rivals blood relatives: sisters in love with the same man, brothers sleeping with the same woman, a son's affair with his stepmother, and a womanizer bouncing between a mother and her daughter. Such stories deliver twice the dramatic punch, breaking hearts and ripping families in half.

MOTHERS AND DAUGHTERS

Tad Martin established his reputation as the town cad when he carried on simultaneous affairs with Liza Colby and her mother, Marian. Marian had recently returned to town after walking out on her family. As such, neither she nor Liza was aware that Tad even knew the other, much less was sleeping with her. Tad not only enjoyed the sex with the far more experienced Marian, he welcomed the gifts that she bought him as thanks for their time together. Liza discovered one of those gifts, a gold chain, and connected Tad to her mother. While Tad was the latest in a long line of young men Marian had lured into bed, Liza had truly fallen in love with Tad. There was no way the story line was going to end on a happy note. After Liza discovered the truth, she slipped into a downward spiral of alcohol and promiscuity. Years later, when Liza returned to town, Marian schemed to reunite her with Tad. Marian also fell into an affair with another of Liza's less than noble exes, Dr. Jonathan Kinder.

A few months before Tad began his affairs with Liza and Marian, a man had come between his mother, Opal, and his sister Jenny. Opal wanted to marry Sam Brady, an electrician, but Sam developed a crush on Opal's daughter Jenny. Although Jenny was head over heels in love with Greg Nelson and didn't return Sam's feelings, Opal blamed her daughter for Sam's lack of interest in getting married.

The corporate-climbing Sean Cudahy was sleeping with Daisy Cortlandt while romantically pursuing her heiress daughter Nina Warner, whose husband Cliff (Peter Bergman) was in jail awaiting trial for murder. Like the rest of Pine Valley, though, Sean did not realize that Daisy, who was calling herself Monique Jonville at the time, was Nina's presumed dead mother. Years later, however, Sean ruined his romance with another young heiress, Cecily Davidson, by letting her catch him kissing her mother, Bitsy.

It took the writers several years to come up with a more sordid triangle than Liza, Tad, and Marian, but in 1995 they succeeded. Alec McIntyre had already established himself as a corporate lothario, trying to steal away Adam Chandler's business and his wife Gloria while Adam was recovering from a car accident. After that affair ran its course, Alec set his sights on Adam's daughter Hayley. Hayley's alcoholic, ex-con mother Arlene in turn set her own sights on Alec. After she discovered that he was stealing money from Hayley's cosmetics company, Arlene blackmailed Alec into an affair. Alec gave into Arlene's blackmail, sleeping with her on his wedding night to Hayley.

FATHERS AND SONS

Natalie Hunter deserves special recognition for coming between two pairs of fathers and sons. When the character was introduced, she was already married to the wealthy Alex Hunter, a rebound relationship that was the result of being dumped by his son Jeremy. When Alex was presumed killed in an avalanche along with Jeremy's lover, Erica Kane, Natalie got Jeremy drunk, slipped into bed with him, and convinced him they had slept together. When Alex and Erica turned up alive, Natalie schemed to trigger Alex's heart condition with a deadly combination of rigorous sex and cigars. Alex died after falling off an ill-tempered horse Natalie had goaded him into riding, and Natalie married Jeremy by claiming that she was pregnant with his child. Although that marriage was illegal, Jeremy and Natalie did marry years down the road after Natalie cleaned up her act.

Natalie wound up playing father against son once again when she got engaged to Palmer Cortlandt, whom she had nursed back to health following a shooting. Palmer's son Ross Chandler didn't trust Natalie; he assumed that she was chasing Palmer for his money. Ross's suspicions soon gave way to lust, and he made love to Natalie. Despite a brief affair with Ross, Natalie went through with the wedding to Palmer. The relationship between Ross and Natalie turned especially nasty after the truth about their affair came out.

An angry and drunken Ross raped Natalie. Refusing to believe that what happened was rape, Palmer disowned Ross and threw Natalie out of the house.

Natalie was not the first woman to come between Palmer and Ross. Palmer was taken in by Ross's gold digger of an ex-wife Cynthia Preston. Shortly after moving into Cortlandt Manor, Cynthia broke up Palmer's marriage to Daisy and took her place as his wife. As much as Cynthia enjoyed Palmer's money and the prestige of being his wife, she still lusted after Ross, who returned the feelings during a business trip.

Just as the gold-digging Natalie Hunter had caused problems between Jeremy Hunter and his father, gold digger Ceara Connor came between Jeremy and his newly discovered son, David Rampal. Ceara didn't return David's affection until she learned that he came from money. Jeremy, who had dealt with Natalie long enough to recognize Ceara for what she was, romanced her away from David for his own good. Ceara naturally took to Jeremy, who had even more money than his son. Along the way, Ceara and Jeremy fell in love, which nearly destroyed Jeremy's already fragile relationship with David.

BROTHERS

Although twins, Adam and Stuart Chandler are miles apart in personality. The kindhearted Stuart Chandler got involved with Gloria Marsh, who had been branded the town trollop because of her affair with the married Craig Lawson. Sure that Gloria was after Stuart's share of the Chandler fortune, Adam pretended to be Stuart to test Gloria's love. When they kissed, Adam and Gloria discovered a mu-

tual attraction. Despite her feelings for Adam, Gloria proceeded with her plans to marry Stuart. And she would have
gone through with it if Stuart had not overheard her and
Adam talking about their affair. Stuart called off the wedding, leaving Gloria free to marry and later divorce Adam.

Edmund Grey and Dimitri Marrick had been rivals long
before they discovered that they were half-brothers. Dimitri
was the heir to the Marrick fortune, and Edmund grew up
as the son of servants on the Marrick estate. Both men fell
in love with Angelique, the housekeeper's daughter, who
eventually married Dimitri. When she emerged from a
coma of many years, she decided that neither man was right
for her and, after a brief affair with Jackson Montgomery,
left town. Years later, after they had mended their problems, Edmund and Dimitri's relationship was ripped in two
once again when Dimitri slept with and presumably impregnated Edmund's wife Maria.

SISTERS

After sleeping her way through the Hunter and Cortlandt
families, it was finally time for Natalie Hunter to see what
it felt like from the other side of an intrafamily love triangle. Her sister Janet Green moved in with Natalie after
escaping an abusive relationship. Janet quickly came to
envy her sister's life: Natalie lived in a mansion; she was
wealthy and engaged to Trevor Dillon, with whom Janet
was falling in love. When Janet's attempt to seduce Trevor
failed, she schemed to take over Natalie's life. Janet lost
weight, bleached her hair, and was tattooed with a birth-
mark identical to one Natalie had on her leg. She dumped
Natalie into an abandoned well and left her to die. Janet's

Natalie Hunter (Kate Collins) was imprisoned in a well by her sister Janet Green. 1991/Cathy Blaivas

charade lasted long enough for her to sleep with Trevor and conceive a child. Years after Natalie's death, Trevor found himself reluctantly attracted to his ex-sister-in-law. Janet also slept with Natalie's ex-husband Palmer Cortlandt in order to blackmail him.

Although Connie Wilkes was only posing as Erica's sister Silver, Erica's lover Kent Bogard did not know that when he began his affair with her. At first, Erica could not even imagine the mousy woman who showed up on her doorstep as any sort of threat to her relationship with Kent. After a beauty salon turned Silver into a sexpot, the playboy in Kent happily added her to his long list of conquests. Silver, like Erica, wanted more than a fling. Neither sister led him down the aisle, as Erica accidentally shot him dead after catching the two of them together in his hotel room.

Death Valley

WHO SHOT JASON MAXWELL? (1973)

Agent Jason Maxwell withheld modeling assignments from
Erica Kane until she agreed to sleep with him. Erica soon
fell for Jason and decided to divorce her husband, Jeff Martin.
One night, Jason called up Jeff and invited him to his
hotel room for a talk. When Jeff got there, he found Jason
shot to death. Jeff was arrested and went on trial for the
murder. His lawyer and uncle, Paul Martin, discovered that
the gun used to kill Jason had belonged to Margo Flax, a
former model and lover of Jason Maxwell; she had bought
the gun intending to shoot Jason for the way he had treated
her, but someone else did Jason in. The writers shocked
the audience with the revelation that Erica's saintly mother,
Mona Kane, had killed Jason, then blocked the murder out
of her mind. With the help of sodium pentathol, Mona remembered
going to Jason's room to order him out of
Erica's life. An arrogant Jason had shoved Margo's gun
into Mona's hand. During the ensuing struggle, the gun

went off, killing Jason. Jeff was cleared, and Mona was not charged with murder.

WHO KILLED EDDIE DORRANCE? (1979)

Almost everyone in town wanted Eddie Dorrance dead. Eddie was supplying drugs to singer Kelly Cole to keep her under his control. He had also raped Brooke English. He was blackmailing con man Langley Wallingford about his past and Phoebe Tyler about her affair with Langley. Kelly Cole was arrested for Eddie's murder, which was committed while she was strung out on drugs. Even she was not sure of her own innocence. Her lover Lincoln Tyler defended her, but she was found guilty of the murder and sentenced to death. Her life was saved by the deathbed confession of Claudette Montgomery, who had shot Eddie after catching him stealing money from the Chateau. Lincoln and Kelly celebrated her freedom by getting married.

WHO KILLED SYBIL THORNE? (1981)

During one of Cliff and Nina's breakups, Cliff fell into bed with nurse Sybil Thorne, who told Cliff on his wedding day to Nina that she was pregnant with his child. Sybil played games with the baby, offering to let Cliff and Nina raise the boy, then reneging on the deal. Palmer Cortlandt used Sybil to drive a wedge between Cliff and Nina. Cliff headed over to Sybil's to have another talk with her and found her dead. He picked up the gun lying beside her, which gave the police a nice copy of his fingerprints on the murder weapon. The situation gave the district attorney's

Sean Cudahy (Alan Dysert, pictured here with Gillian Spencer) killed Sybil Thorne. 1981/Ann Limongello

office more than sufficient motive. During the trial, Monique Jonvil took the stand and testified that she was Daisy Cortlandt, Nina's presumed dead mother. Daisy also testified that her young lover Sean Cudahy had killed Sybil. Sean confessed that under his boss Palmer Cortlandt's orders he had gone over to Sybil's apartment with a gun. He never intended to kill her. He only intended to frighten her into sticking with the original game plan to break Cliff and Nina apart.

WHO KILLED ZACH GRAYSON? (1985)

Con artist–male prostitute Zach Grayson quickly insin-
uated himself into the lives of Pine Valley's wealthiest cit-
izens. He blackmailed Ross Chandler and Cynthia
Cortlandt with information about their adultery. He conned
Tad Martin out of ten thousand dollars. He drugged Nina
Warner and took nude photos of her. When Ross Chandler
walked into Zach's apartment one night in the spring of
1985, he found Nina's mother, Daisy, crouched over Zach's
lifeless body, a bloody knife in her hand. Daisy, who had
been Zach's lover, was convicted of murder and sentenced
to prison. Cliff Warner teamed up with Brooke English to
find the real killer. They discovered that Marian Colby, one
of Zach's former clients, killed him in self-defense.

WHO KILLED WILL CORTLANDT? (1992)

In the spring of 1992, Will Cortlandt began his descent into
hell. He raped nurse Gloria Marsh and married Hayley
Vaughn to get his hands on her money. Nearly the entire
town wanted to get rid of him. When an alcoholic Hayley
finally realized what a monster she had married, she bar-
ricaded herself in her bedroom. Will's plans to forcibly
consummate their marriage were cut short by a crowbar.
Hayley's ex-boyfriend, Brian Bodine, thinking that Hayley
had killed her husband, put his fingerprints all over the
murder weapon and was subsequently charged with the
murder. The real killer, however, turned out to be a pregnant Janet Green, who escaped from her hospital room to
kill Will. Janet killed Will out of her twisted devotion to
Hayley's uncle Trevor. Janet, who was already serving time

for kidnapping her sister Natalie, went back to prison after giving birth.

WHO SHOT LAUREL DILLON? (1995)

After Michael Delaney came out to his high school class, homophobia swept through Pine Valley. Michael defended his case on Tad Martin's talk show, *The Cutting Edge*. Michael's sister Laurel Dillon joined him onstage as a show of support. A shot rang out from the audience, killing Laurel. Suspicion naturally fell on Janet Green, whom the cameras caught holding the murder weapon. Laurel would not have been Janet's first victim; and Janet had previously tried to kill Laurel by cutting the brakes in her car. Janet, however, was not the killer, and Laurel was not the intended victim. The killer, student intern Jason Sheffield, had been aiming at Michael Delaney. Right before the show began, Jason had learned that his younger brother Kevin, one of Michael's students, was gay—a fact that Jason blamed on Michael. Jason confessed his crime to Hayley during an A.A. meeting, expecting that she would be bound to keep his secret. Hayley thought otherwise and revealed Jason's confession during Janet's trial.

Pine Valley's Ten Most Wanted List

All My Children has tended to shy away from the sort of supercriminals that have wreaked their havoc on soap operas such as *General Hospital* and *One Life to Live*. That is not to say that Pine Valley has remained exactly crime-free. In the following quiz, see how well you can identify each criminal from his—or her—signature crimes. (Answers on page 199.)

1. _____ raped Ruth Martin and was later killed by a bomb he built himself to kill her entire family.

2. A pimp, _____, tried to bury one of his former prositutes alive.

3. Also known as Cobra, _____ forced her own stepdaughter to smuggle drugs.

4. _____ supplied Erica Kane with drugs and

Master crimnal Billy Clyde Tuggle (Matthew Cowles) developed an ob-
session with Dixie Cooney (Cady McClain). 1990/Cathy Blaivas

kept Skye Chandler sedated for almost a year while he
drained her bank account.

5. _____ sold drugs to children and raped
Julia Santos.

6. Cult leader _____ tried to brainwash Silver Kane into killing her half-sister Erica.

7. A wife beater, _____ torched Trevor Dillon's home and then kidnapped his wife, Natalie, who was
blinded in the fire.

8. Cosmetics executive _____ tried to kill
Erica Kane and Palmer Cortlandt to keep his past as a Nazi
war criminal secret.

9. Con artist _____ tricked Phoebe Tyler Wallingford into marriage, then left town disguised as a woman after trying to kill his wife.

10. Hollywood actor _____ had raped Erica Kane on her fourteenth birthday and years later went after Erica's young daughter Bianca.

Facts About the Stars

EDUCATION

Current head writer Lorraine Broderick was Michael E. Knight's (*Tad Martin*) freshman dean at Wesleyan University.

In high school Susan Lucci (*Erica Kane*) went to Norway as an exchange student.

While in high school, Tricia Pursley (*Devon McFadden*) trained with Ringling Bros./Barnum and Bailey Circus.

Richard Van Vleet (*Dr. Chuck Tyler*) took thirty years to finish his college education. He was the keynote speaker at his graduation from Western State College.

Rudolf Martin (*Anton Lang*), who was born in Germany, speaks not only English and German but French and Italian as well.

David Canary (*Adam and Stuart Chandler*), Shari Headley (*Mimi Reed*), and Jean LeClerc (*Jeremy Hunter*) all enrolled in premed programs in college.

In between her roles on *All My Children* and *Days of Our Lives*, Hunter Tylo (*Robin McCall*) took premed courses at Fordham University.

Kathleen Noone (*Ellen Shepherd*) holds a master's degree in fine arts.

Steve Kanaly (*Seabone Hunkle*) went to school with Sally Field, Stacy Keach, and Tom Selleck.

At Northwestern, Agnes Nixon's fellow students in the drama program included future Oscar winners Charlton Heston and Patricia Neal.

Elizabeth Lawrence (*Myra Murdoch*), who holds a master of science degree in special education, worked as a teacher in between her roles on *A World Apart* and *All My Children*.

John Callahan (*Edmund Grey*) studied prelaw at the University of California, Berkeley.

Christopher Lawford (*Charlie Brent*) graduated from Boston College Law School. He failed to pass the bar on his first attempt and never tried again.

NAMES

Maurice Benard (*Nico Kelly*) named one of his pet cats Nico after his role on the show.

Days of Our Lives Emmy winner Leann Hunley was named after Lee Meriwether (*Ruth Martin*), who used to be known as Lee Ann.

While growing up, Cady McClain (*Dixie Cooney*) went by her middle name Jo, which is what her closest friends still call her.

Nick Benedict (*Phil Brent*) took to calling his on-screen mother Mary Fickett "Mom" both on and off the show.

Robin Christopher's (*Skye Chandler*) mother picked out her first name when a robin flew in her hospital room window shortly after she gave birth.

Dondre Whitfield (*Terrence Frye*) was originally going to be named Andre, but his mother decided that it had become too common among children. So she tinkered around with it and came up with Dondre.

The initials in T. C. Warner's (*Kelsey Jefferson*) name don't stand for anything. Warner's parents just liked the way they sounded.

LIVING ARRANGEMENTS

T. C. Warner (*Kelsey Jefferson*) grew up without a TV in the house.

Matthew Cowles (*Billy Clyde Tuggle*) refuses to keep a TV set in his house.

Alla Korot (*Dr. Allie Doyle*) was born in Odessa, Russia. She came to America at age six.

Eileen Herlie (*Myrtle Fargate*) was born in Glasgow, Scotland.

Mark Consuelos (*Mateo Santos*) was born in Spain.

Peter Bergman (*Dr. Cliff Warner*) was born on the naval base on Guantánamo Bay in Cuba.

Trent Bushey continued living at the YMCA after landing his role as David Rampal.

All My Children fan Rosie O'Donnell used to live in the same building as Michael E. Knight (*Tad Martin*). On one elevator ride, she was talking about how cute he was, unaware that the blond woman sharing the elevator with her was Catherine Hickland, Knight's wife.

Andrew Jackson (*Dr. Stephen Hammill*) lived in the

apartment above Madonna's but rarely saw her, since they rode different elevators. His plumbing did, however, leak into her bedroom.

Sydney Penny (*Julia Santos*) lived in David Letterman's old apartment building. Letterman stopped by her apartment one day while filming a segment on the building's new tenants. He walked around the apartment and checked out her closets, but neither Penny nor her apartment made it onto his show.

SPORTS

Chris Bruno (*Michael Delaney*) plays on a semipro baseball team known as The National Network. He used to play with another semipro team, the Long Island White Sox.

Michael Sabatino (*Dr. Jonathan Kinder*) tried out as a pole vaulter for the 1976 U.S. Olympic Team.

David Canary (*Adam and Stuart Chandler*) is the assistant coach of his son's Little League baseball team.

John Callahan (*Edmund Grey*) competes in ten to twelve pro-am golf tournaments a year.

Sarah Michelle Gellar (*Kendall Hart*) learned to skate at the age of three. She came in third place in a New York regional competition. She also came in fourth place in her division in a karate championship at Madison Square Garden.

An avid runner, William Christian (*Derek Frye*) has finished the New York marathon.

Kathleen Noone's (*Ellen Shepard*) father played baseball with the Brooklyn Dodgers.

Walt Willey's (*Jackson Montgomery*) father played with the St. Louis Cardinals farm team. A car accident that shattered Willey's leg when he was twelve prevented him from following in his father's footsteps.

RELIGION

Jill Larson (*Opal Gardner*) is legally ordained to perform wedding ceremonies. Among the couples she has joined in holy matrimony have been her own sister and brother-in-law.

Peter White (*Lincoln Tyler*) studied to be an Episcopalian minister.

Every year, Eva LaRue Callahan (*Dr. Maria Santos*) engages in a ten-day religious fast.

A devoted fan of radio serials when she was growing up, *All My Children* creator Agnes Nixon once gave up listening to the *Little Orphan Annie* show for Lent.

Judith Barcroft's (*Ann Tyler*) father was a minister who performed a funeral on *Another World* when she was on the show.

MILITARY EXPERIENCE

David Canary (*Adam and Stuart Chandler*) was named Best Pop Singer in an All Army Contest.

Richard Lawson (*Lucas Barnes*) was a combat medic in Vietnam.

Nicholas Coster (*Steve Andrews*) is a licensed skipper with the U.S. Coast Guard.

Ray MacDonnell (*Joe Martin*) was a radar technician in the navy.

Elizabeth Lawrence (*Myra Murdoch*) served with the

James Mitchell (seen dancing here with Ruth Warrick as Phoebe Tyler) began his career as a dancer. 1980/Steve Fenn

WAVES. During World War II, she worked as an airplane mechanic and a celestial navigation instructor.

Steve Kanaly's (*Seabone Hunkle*) duty as a radio operator in Vietnam led to a friendship with screenwriter John Milius. Kanaly served as a technical advisor on Milius's screenplay for *Apocalypse Now*. Kanaly's helicopter unit served as the basis for the unit headed up by Robert Duvall in the Francis Ford Coppola film.

OTHER JOBS

Peter Bergman (*Dr. Cliff Warner*) worked as a bricklayer.
Susan Lucci (Erica Kane) worked as a color girl for

CBS. The job consisted of sitting on a stool while technicians developed a system of lighting for color television.

Winsor Harmon (*Del Henry*) was the Marlboro man in South America.

Darlene Dahl (*Anita Santos*) sanded floors.

Agnes Nixon's father wanted her to join the family mortuary business.

A licensed pilot, Richard Van Vleet (*Chuck Tyler*) has worked as a crop duster. Van Vleet has also worked as a stuntman, appearing on such TV series as *Ironside* and *To Catch a Thief.*

Robin Christopher (*Skye Chandler*) worked as a model and has appeared on the cover of several romance novels.

As a telephone repair supervisor, Amelia Marshall (*Belinda Keefer*) has climbed her share of telephone poles.

Daniel Cosgrove (*Scott Chandler*) worked as a bailiff in the Sheriff's Office of New Haven County, Connecticut.

Michael Sabatino's (*Dr. Jonathan Kinder*) first job, at the age of eight, was feeding calf hearts to his neighbor's owl.

Even while working on *All My Children*, Elizabeth Lawrence (*Myra Murdoch*) volunteered her time as a member of the New York auxiliary police department. Among her varied duties, she worked as a crossing guard.

Chris Bruno (*Michael Delaney*) owns a martini bar in Manhattan called Vermouth. His co-owners include his brother Dylan and three guys who fired him from his first bartending job.

Michael Nader (*Dimitri Marrick*) was working as a caterer in between acting gigs. He learned that he won the role of Dex Dexter on *Dynasty* during a job, at which point he handed in his apron.

CELEBRITY ENCOUNTERS

Part-time stand-up comic Walt Willey (*Jackson Montgomery*) ran into Milton Berle at the airport. Willey gave the legendary comedian a Monte Cristo cigar, in return for which Berle gave Willey a joke to use in his act.

Lisa Ann Walters, star of the ABC sitcom *Life's Work*, used to open for Walt Willey's stand-up act.

Warren Burton (*Eddie Dorrance*) wrote club acts for Lily Tomlin and Joan Rivers.

Deborah Goodrich (*Connie Wilkes*) was a bridesmaid when Julia Roberts married singer Lyle Lovett.

Susan Lucci (*Erica Kane*) attended the Jacqueline Kennedy Onasis auction. She bought her son Andreas lapel pins that John F. Kennedy and Jackie had collected from the various countries they visited as First Couple. For her daughter Liza, she bought a sketch of a leopard.

Michael E. Knight (*Tad Martin*) and his wife, Catherine Hickland, collect Hollywood memorabilia. Among the pieces they have bought are a signed photograph of Charlie Chaplin and a canceled check signed by Clark Gable.

MUSICAL TALENT

Nicholas Benedict (*Phil Brent*) played drums professionally in a number of Las Vegas lounges.

Darnell Williams (*Jesse Hubbard*) released an album called *Pure Satisfaction*. His leading lady Debbi Morgan (*Angie Hubbard*) sang with him on one cut.

Michael Sabatino (*Dr. Jonathan Kinder*) can play the accordion.

Jill Larson (*Opal Gardner Cortlandt*) plays the saxophone.

In the mid '60s, Michael Minor (*Brandon Kingsley*) released a pair of albums, *This Is Mike Minor!* and *Silver Dollar—Ace in the Hole.* Between 1959 and 1973, he also recorded a dozen singles.

While Rosemary Prinz (*Amy Tyler*) was playing Penny Hughes on *As the World Turns,* she released the album *TV's Penny Sings,* as well as the single "Penny."

In 1981, John Wesley Shipp (*Carter Jones*) released the album *Images.*

Rosa Nevin (*Cecily Davidson*) and her husband Gerald have recorded an album together under the group name Gerosa.

Kathleen Noone (*Ellen Shepherd*) plays the trombone and sang with the Jimmy Dorsey Orchestra.

Felicity LaFortune (*Laurel Banning*) stopped pursuing a career in opera after developing nodes on her vocal cords.

THE TONY AWARDS

Mary Fickett (*Ruth Martin*) was nominated for a Tony Award in 1958 for *Sunrise at Campobello,* which won the award for Best Drama.

Eileen Herlie (*Myrtle Fargate*) competed against future *All My Children* fan and guest star Carol Burnett for the 1960 Tony for Best Actress in a Musical. Herlie had co-starred with Jackie Gleason in *Take Me Along;* Burnett starred in *Once Upon a Mattress.* They both lost to Broadway legend Mary Martin for *The Sound of Music.*

In 1989, Brian L. Green (*Brian Bodine*) was nominated as Best Actor in a Musical for *Starmites.*

In 1976, Robert LuPone (*Zach Grayson*) was nominated for a Tony Award for *A Chorus Line*, in which he played a character named Zach.

Tonya Pinkins (*Livia Frye*) juggled her work on *All My Children* with a role in *Jelly's Last Jam*, which earned her the 1992 Tony as Best Supporting or Featured Actress in a Musical. She was recently nominated for a second Tony as Best Actress in the musical *Play On!*

While known as a comic actress, Anne Meara (*Peggy Moody*) earned a Tony nomination as Best Featured Actress in a Drama for her work in the 1993 revival of *Anna Christie*.

Lynne Thigpen (*Grace Keefer*) won the 1997 Tony as Best Featured Actress in a Drama for her work in Wendy Wasserstein's *An American Daughter*. She had been nominated in 1981 as Best Featured Actress in a Musical for *Tintypes*.

Larry Keith (*Nick Davis*) played Isidor Strauss in the Broadway play *Titanic*, which won the 1997 Tony for Best Musical.

BEAUTY PAGEANTS

Lee Meriwether (*Ruth Martin*) was crowned Miss America in 1955, the first time that the pageant was broadcast on television.

Courtney Eplin (*Galen Henderson*) is a former Miss USA.

As a child, Eva LaRue Callahan (*Dr. Maria Santos*) was named Little Miss California. She was one of the top ten finalists in the Little Miss World pageant.

Hunter Tylo (*Robin McCall*) was named Miss Fort Worth.

Alla Korot (*Dr. Allie Doyle*) was named Miss California T.E.E.N.

As a teenager, Susan Lucci (*Erica Kane*) made it into the semifinals of the New York State Miss Universe pageant but had to drop out of the contest to take her final exams at college.

Teresa Blake's (*Gloria Marsh*) modeling career began after she won a bikini contest sponsored by Hawaiian Tropic.

Esta Terblanche (*Gillian*) was named Miss Teen South Africa in 1991.

John Callahan (*Edmund Grey*) and Eva LaRue Callahan co-hosted the 1997 Miss America pageant.

SUPER-HEROICS

Lee Meriwether played a love interest for Bruce Wayne in the 1960s live-action *Batman* TV series. In the feature film adaptation of the show, Meriwether took on the role of arch-criminal Catwoman.

Two other *All My Children* actors tangled with the Dynamic Duo back in the '60s. Malachi Throne (*Morgan Rutherford*) played the villainous master of disguise False Face, and Barbara Rush (*Nola Orsini*) played Nora Clavicle, a corrupt women's libber who stole Commissioner Gordon's job.

Melody Anderson (*Natalie Dillon*) played Flash Gordon's girlfriend Dale Arden in the 1980 feature film.

John Wesley Shipp, who played Galen Henderson's physically abusive ex-husband (*Carter Jones*), had played the super-fast crimefighter, The Flash, in the TV show of the same name, which was adapted from the comic book.

Ray MacDonnell (*Joe Martin*, seen here with Mary Fickett as *Ruth*) once filmed the pilot to play Dick Tracy in a TV series. 1991/Donna Svennevik

In the very first episode, Michael Nader (*Dimitri Marrick*) played the villain.

Alla Korot (*Dr. Allie Doyle*) was the model for Esmeralda in Disney's animated film *The Hunchback of Notre Dame*.

Comic book collector Trent Bushey (*David Rampal*) came very close to landing the lead role in the syndicated TV series *Superboy* until one of the producers decided that he didn't like the shape of Bushey's chin.

SOAP ACTORS PLAYING SOAP ACTORS

On *Fantasy Island*, Susan Lucci (*Erica Kane*) played a soap opera actress who feared that her TV alter ego was taking over her life.

In the 1982 TV movie *Fantasies*, Peter Bergman (*Cliff Warner*) and Robin Mattson (*Janet Green*) played castmates who were done in by a serial killer preying upon soap actors.

Judith Barcroft (*Ann Tyler Martin*) played Barbara Wilde on *Ryan's Hope*'s soap-within-a-soap *The Proud and the Passionate*.

Keith Hamilton Cobb (*Noah Keefer*) played a soap star in an episode of *The Fresh Prince of Bel Air*.

Steve Caffrey (*Andrew Cortlandt*) played a gay soap opera actor in the film *Longtime Companion*.

Maxwell Caulfield filmed his role as a soap actor in the feature film *Blonde Ambition* before landing the role of Pierce Riley.

Kelly Ripa (*Hayley Vaughn*) and John Callahan (*Edmund Grey*) were paired romantically as characters in a soap opera in the Meryl Streep–Robert DeNiro film *Marvin's Room*. Ripa's castmates Teresa Blake (*Gloria Marsh*) and Eva LaRue Callahan (*Dr. Maria Santos*) also auditioned for her role.

Elizabeth Lawrence (*Myra Murdoch*) played a soap opera writer based on the legendary Irna Phillips in the daytime serial *A World Apart*.

THE CUTTING ROOM FLOOR

At the age of eleven, T. C. Warner (*Kelsey Jefferson*) was hired for her first film, the Kevin Costner Western *Silverado*, but her scenes were never used.

Tommy J. Michaels (*Timmy Dillon*) was seen playing a cub scout in the previews for the Oscar-nominated *Quiz*

Show, but his scene didn't make its way into the final product.

While Ben Monk (*Kevin Sheffield*) was seen in the background of the Leonardo DiCaprio drama *The Basketball Diaries*, he was not heard. His two lines of dialogue were cut from the film.

Michael Nader (*Dimitri Marrick*) was cut out of the Richard Gere–Kim Basinger thriller *Final Analysis*.

James Patrick Stuart (*Will Cortlandt*) was not completely edited out of the Richard Gere–Julia Roberts romance *Pretty Woman*, but the majority of the work he'd filmed was.

MISCELLANEOUS

Keith Hamilton Cobb (*Noah Keefer*) hasn't cut his hair since 1986.

Walt Willey (*Jackson Montgomery*) stuttered as a child.

Susan Lucci (*Erica Kane*) hates to watch herself on TV with other people in the room. She has therefore installed a television set next to her tub so she can watch herself in private while enjoying a long bath.

A fan of the Curious George books as a child, Lonnie Quinn (*Will Cooney*) owned a pet monkey for three years.

As a child, Hunter Tylo (*Robin McCall*) had a thing for reptiles. Among her pets were boa constrictors and baby alligators.

Cady McClain (*Dixie Cooney*) made *The Guiness Book of World Records* as part of the largest tap dancing routine. There were five hundred tap dancers involved.

Richard Lawson (*Lucas Barnes*) has survived two car crashes and a plane crash as well.

A psychic told Kelly Ripa's (*Hayley Vaughn*) younger sister that her older sister would land a role on a soap opera in two years. The sisters Ripa laughed about the prediction until it came true.

Happy Birthday to Them

January

22 Brian Gaskill (*Bobby Warner*)
26 Walt Willey (*Jackson Montgomery*)
28 Keith Hamilton Cobb (*Noah Keefer*)

February

8 Julia Barr (*Brooke English*)
8 Tommy J. Michaels (*Tim Dillon*)
18 Michael Nader (*Dimitri Marrick*)
29 James Mitchell (*Palmer Cortlandt*)

March

1 Richard Shoberg (*Tom Cudahy*)
5 Ray MacDonnell (*Joe Martin*)
5 T. C. Warner (*Kelsey Jefferson*)

8	Eileen Herlie (*Myrtle Fargate*)
15	Chris Bruno (*Michael Delaney*)
20	Michael Lowry (*Jake Martin*)
29	Christopher Lawford (*Charlie Brent*)
30	Mark Consuelos (*Mateo Santos*)

April

2	Amelia Marshall (*Belinda Keefer*)
14	Sarah Michelle Gellar (*Kendall Hart*)
24	Shane McDermott (*Scott Chandler*)
27	Ingrid Rogers (*Taylor Roxbury-Cannon*)
27	Susan Pratt (*Barbara Montgomery*)

May

7	Michael E. Knight (*Tad Martin*)
23	Mary Fickett (*Ruth Martin*)
27	Dondre T. Whitfield (*Terrence Frye*)
27	Lee Meriwether (*Ruth Martin*)
30	Tonya Pinkins (*Livia Frye*)

June

1	Robin Mattson (*Janet Green*)
25	Michael Sabatino (*Dr. Jonathan Kinder*)
29	Ruth Warrick (*Phoebe Tyler Wallingford*)

Tad Martin (Michael E. Knight) with one of his three mothers, Opal Gardner (Dorothy Lyman). 1989/Ann Limongello

July
6 James Kiberd (*Trevor Dillon*)
22 Jennifer Bassey (*Marian Colby*)
29 Shari Headley (*Mimi Reed*)
29 Kelli Taylor (*Taylor Roxbury-Cannon*)
30 Ben Monk (*Kevin Sheffield*)
31 Rudolf Martin (*Anton Lang*)

August
6 Grant Aleksander (*Alec McIntyre*)
7 Sydney Penny (*Julia Santos*)

9   Gina Gallagher (*Bianca Montgomery*)
25   David Canary (*Adam and Stuart Chandler*)

September

18   Carrie Genzel (*Skye Chandler*)
22   Anne Meara (*Peggy Moody*)
24   Louis Edmonds (*Langley Wallingford*)
25   Alexis Manta (*Amanda Dillon*)
30   William Christian (*Derek Frye*)

October

1   Darlene Dahl (*Anita Santos*)
2   Kelly Ripa (*Hayley Vaughan*)
7   Jill Larson (*Opal Gardner Cortlandt*)
13   Cady McClain (*Dixie Martin*)

November

1   Alla Korot (*Dr. Allie Doyle*)
22   Winsor Harmon (*Del Henry*)
24   Roscoe Born (*Jim Thomasen*)
26   Marcy Walker (*Liza Colby*)

December

2   Eva LaRue Callahan (*Dr. Maria Santos*)
3   Melody Anderson (*Natalie Dillon*)

3   Lauren Roman (*Laura Kirk*)
6   Lindsay Price (*An-Li Chen*)
12   Teresa Blake (*Gloria Marsh*)
15   Felicity LaFortune (*Laurel Banning*)
16   Daniel Cosgrove (*Scott Chandler*)
22   Lynne Thigpen (*Grace Keefer*)
23   Susan Lucci (*Erica Kane*)
23   John Callahan (*Edmund Grey*)

Casting Stories

Ruth Warrick, who had played Edith Hughes on *As the World Turns* in the late '50s, heard about *All My Children* through Rosemary Prinz, who had played Edith's niece Penny on the show. Warrick contacted Nixon, who was reluctant at first to hire her. In her early fifties, Warrick was too young to play either of the show's grandmothers, Kate Martin or Phoebe Tyler, both of whom were old enough to have grandchildren in their late teens. Warrick convinced Nixon that with trips to the beauty salon and health spas, many grandmothers were looking much younger than they had in the past. She also suggested that Phoebe's "grandson" Chuck could be a step-grandson; Phoebe could have been Charles Tyler's second wife. Nixon made the necessary changes to hire Warrick. Unfortunately, James Karen, the actor who was first cast to play Phoebe's son Lincoln, was replaced shortly into the show's run because he was suddenly too old to be playing Phoebe's son.

It is nearly impossible for most *All My Children* fans to imagine a Pine Valley without Susan Lucci as Erica

Ruth Warrick (pictured here with Louis Edmonds) had a successful film career before coming to daytime. 1979/Steve Fenn

Kane. Yet, Susan Lucci almost didn't try out for the show because it was raining the day the auditions were being held. And when she got there, she didn't audition for Erica but for Tara, the show's sweet young heroine. Line producer Bud Kloss, who was conducting the preliminary auditions, was immediately taken with Lucci's presence and brought her in to meet executive producer Doris Quinlan, promising her that he had found Tara. After watching Lucci read for the part, Quinlan informed Kloss that Lucci was definitely a find, but she was not Tara; she was Erica.

Agnes Nixon wanted Ray MacDonnell for the role of Dr. Joe Martin after she saw his work on *The Edge of Night*, where he played lawyer Phil Capice. She offered him the role without an audition. Procter & Gamble graciously let MacDonnell out of his contract so that he could star on *All My Children*.

The casting director and producer were not that interested in Charles Frank when he auditioned for the role of Jeff Martin. They both agreed that his voice sounded too nasal. When Agnes Nixon saw him, she felt as if she were looking at Jeff Martin. So she hired him and paid for him to take voice lessons before the show premiered.

When Charles Frank left, Agnes Nixon decided to recast the role of Jeff. Among the actors who auditioned for the role was Mark LaMura. Although Nixon didn't see LaMura as Jeff, she thought that he could be a valuable addition to the show. The role of music teacher Mark Dalton was created for him and named after him as well.

Patricia Barry used to live across the street from the studio where *All My Children* once taped. As such, she always thought it would be convenient to land a role on the soap. And she did—three weeks after she moved back to California, where she had gone to look for work. The show offered her the role of Brooke English's mother, Peg. Barry told the producers that she would accept as long as the role was a sweet one. She was in the midst of planning her daughter's wedding and didn't want any dark story lines overshadowing her. Shortly after signing on, Barry started receiving scripts revealing that Peg was an international drug smuggler.

From the very beginning of her soap opera career, Marcy Walker was a much sought after young actress. She was offered roles on both *All My Children* and *As the World Turns*. She, of course, picked *All My Children*.

Michael E. Knight was so nervous the day that he went in to screen-test for the role of troublemaker Tad Martin that his hands were shaking. Rather than let the producers see his hands shake, he kept them in the pockets of his leather bomber jacket throughout the entire scene. The producers liked the sort of attitude that gesture conveyed and hired him for the role.

Jennifer Bassey did not need to audition for the role of Marian Colby. Francesca James, who was directing *All My Children* in the early '80s, met Bassey at a wedding and liked her look. James introduced her to producer Jacqueline Babbin, who hired her for what was originally intended to be a five-month role.

All My Children was having a difficult time recasting the role of Brian Bodine when producer Felicia Minei Behr caught Matt Borlenghi on an episode of the police drama *Hunter*. Although Borlenghi's spot lasted only thirty seconds, it was long enough to make an impression on Behr, who decided that he was Brian.

Lindsay Price was living in California when she got the call to audition for the role of An-Li Chen, which she did in ABC's Los Angeles studio. Her parents did not tell Price that the soap opera was produced in New York City. They were afraid she wouldn't go to the audition if she realized getting the role would require that she relocate to the other side of the country.

While flipping through a soap opera magazine, Eva LaRue's (*Dr. Maria Santos*) then husband John O'Hurley pointed to a picture and said, "There's another picture of you.'' The picture, as it turned out, was of Sydney Penny, who was starring on *Santa Barbara* at the time. The resemblance between La Rue and Penny was so close that it took even LaRue a moment to realize that it wasn't she. LaRue and her husband were obviously not the only ones to notice the resemblance. A few weeks later, Penny was cast in the role of Maria's younger sister Julia.

Richard Roland was cast in the part of Jason Sheffield, the college student who falls for older woman Dixie Martin (Cady McClain). Although the age difference between the characters was not that great, the story line was played out as a younger man infatuated with an older woman. In reality, however, Roland is older than McClain.

While many soaps cast actors in their twenties to play high school students, Sarah Michelle Gellar was only fifteen when she landed the role of twentysomething Kendall Hart.

Of the five soap opera roles Robin Mattson has played throughout her career, she has not originated a single one of them. She was *Guiding Light*'s fifth Hope Bauer, *General Hospital*'s third Heather Webber, *Ryan's Hope*'s fourth Delia Reid, *Santa Barbara*'s second Gina Capwell, and *All My Children*'s second Janet Green.

Some of the best-known actors in soaps right now have auditioned for roles on *All My Children*. Phil Carey tried out for the part of Palmer Cortlandt shortly before landing the role of billionaire cowboy Asa Buchanan on *One Life to Live*. Carey's castmate, five-time Emmy winner Erika Slezak, had auditioned for the role of Mary Kennicott; whether she would have landed the role will never be known since she took her name out of the running when *One Life to Live* hired her to play Victoria Lord Riley.

A number of famous faces have auditioned for *All My*

Children through the years. Juliana Marguiles, who has won an Emmy for playing a nurse on the prime-time drama *E.R.*, had auditioned for the role of Dr. Maria Santos. And Brendan Fraser, who has starred in such films as *School Ties* and *George of the Jungle*, read for the part of Brian Bodine when *All My Children* was recasting the role.

Oscar nominee Julia Roberts, who went on to become one of Hollywood's most popular actresses in films such as *Pretty Woman* and *My Best Friend's Wedding*, had screen-tested for the role of Cliff Warner's troublemaking sister Linda. During that screen test, Bill Timoney, who played Alfred Vanderpoole, filled in for Tad.

PRE-*Child*HOOD

Over the years, *All My Children* has attracted some of the finest actors on daytime, many of whom have proven themselves on other shows. In the following puzzle, match up the current cast members with their previous soap roles. Answers on page 199.

1.	John Callahan *(Edmund Grey)*	a.	Gilly Grant, *Guiding Light*
2.	Marcy Walker *(Liza Colby)*	b.	Nick Rivers, *The City*
3.	Ray MacDonnell *(Dr. Joe Martin)*	c.	Edith Hughes, *As the World Turns*
4.	Ruth Warrick *(Phoebe Tyler Wallingford)*	d.	Julian Hatthaway, *Where the Heart Is*
5.	David Canary *(Adam and Stuart Chandler)*	e.	Ursula Blackwell, *One Life to Live*

6. Alla Korot
   (*Dr. Allie Doyle*)
7. Roscoe Born
   (*Jim Thomasen*)
8. Julia Barr
   (*Brooke English*)
9. James Mitchell
   (*Palmer Cortlandt*)
10. Jill Larson
    (*Opal Gardner*)
11. James Kiberd
    (*Trevor Dillon*)
12. Amelia Marshall
    (*Belinda Keefer*)

f. Leo Russell,
   General Hospital
g. Eden Capwell,
   Santa Barbara
h. Far Wind,
   The Doctors
i. Reenie Szabo,
   Ryan's Hope
j. Mike Donovan,
   Loving
k. Jenna Norris,
   Another World
l. Phil Capice,
   The Edge of Night

Double Duty

When Francesca James decided to leave *All My Children* to pursue her career in music, Kitty Shea, her character, died from a brain tumor. At the going-away party, James expressed to Agnes Nixon her fears about leaving the show. Nixon, who had always wanted to do a twin story line, assured James that she would always be welcome back. Because of the audience's distress over Kitty's death and James's homesickness, Kitty's long-lost twin sister Kelly Cole arrived in Pine Valley only a few months after Kitty's death. Kelly was harder than Kitty but troubled in her own way, as she was addicted to pills. Linc Tyler, who had loved Kitty, fell even harder for her twin sister. The role of Kelly earned James an Emmy.

Agnes Nixon got to do the ultimate twin story line with Adam and Stuart Chandler, both of whom have been played by David Canary since 1983. When the character of Adam was first introduced, the audience was not let in on the fact that Adam had a twin brother. It wasn't until Adam burst into the attic where Stuart was kept and prevented his

David Canary as twins Adam and Stuart Chandler. 1996/ABC

brother from killing Ellen Shepherd that the audience discovered Adam's secret. Since that time, Canary has been given an acting range few actors have enjoyed on one show. He has been able to add in nuances such as Adam pretending to be Stuart and vice versa. For his efforts, Canary has been rewarded with four Emmys.

While Adam has been given the lion's share of the plot lines, one of the show's best love stories featured Stuart and Cindy Parker, a young mother dying from AIDS. Playing Cindy was Ellen Wheeler, who herself had won an Emmy the year before for playing twin sisters on *Another World*—the same year that Canary won the first of his four Emmys for playing Adam and Stuart. Although the story line dictated that Cindy had to die, the producers hated losing a talented actress like Wheeler. Shortly before Cindy died, the show introduced her look-alike sister Karen. The evil Karen didn't click with the audience the way that Cindy had, and the character was written off after kidnapping Adam Chandler Junior.

The show's most entertaining pair of look-alike sisters has been Natalie Hunter and Janet Green, both played by Kate Collins. When Kate Collins debuted on *All My Children*, Natalie was the villainess, a spider woman who tried to "love" her heart patient husband to death while pursuing his son Jeremy. By the time Natalie had transformed into one of the show's leading heroines, the writers introduced Natalie's overweight, brunette sister Janet. Obsessed with Natalie's fiancé Trevor Dillon, Janet lost weight, bleached her hair, and stole Natalie's life. Natalie lay in the bottom of a well while Janet, disguised as Natalie, married Trevor and got pregnant by him. The role of Janet gave Collins the chance to showcase her talent for humor.

Among Janet's various crimes, she murdered Will Cortlandt. Will's murder did not, however, end James Patrick Stuart's association with *All My Children*. Several years after Will's death, Stuart returned to the show as Justin Carrier, an actor whom Janet Green paid to impersonate Will's ghost—part of a scheme to derail Will's sister Dixie from her quest to drive Janet out of Pine Valley. While not in Will makeup, the character of Justin was played by James Garde, who bore more than a passing resemblance to James Patrick Stuart. Garde originally came to the attention of the show when he auditioned for the role of Dixie's other brother, Del Henry. The dual casting of Garde and Stuart as the same character presented the two actors with the challenge of keeping their mannerisms and speech patterns as uniform as possible.

Stuart and Garde pulled off playing the same character

Kate Collins played Natalie Hunter and her psychotic sister Janet Green.
1991/ABC

so well that even the producers had a hard time telling them
apart. Garde was woken up at eight o'clock one morning
by the show wondering where he was. Garde, who thought
that he had the day off, pulled himself out of bed and hur-
ried down to the studio, which was only a few blocks from
his house. As soon as Garde showed up on the set, the
producers realized that it was Stuart they needed for the
day's shooting.

In 1983, Lynne Thigpen had a short-term role as Flora,
the aunt with whom Angie Hubbard stayed while she was
pregnant. Ten years later, Thigpen rejoined the show as
Grace Keefer, who stole police officer Mimi Reed's baby
to get even with Mimi for killing her son during a robbery
attempt. After some time in an institution, Grace has been

During Christmas of 1996, Myrtle (Eileen Herlie) fell in love with Santa Claus (Clifton James). 1996/ABC

reformed and has been playing aunt on a recurring basis to Noah and Belinda Keefer.

An amnesiac, Tad Martin returned to Pine Valley in 1993 believing that he was Ted Orsini, the heir to a vineyard who had been kidnapped as a child many years previously. Shortly after Tad regained his memory, the real Ted Orsini showed up in town. Michael E. Knight took on the role of Ted. Unlike the comic and dramatic Tad, Ted was laconic and played his emotions very close to the vest. Tad bent over backward trying to return to Ted what was rightfully his, but what Ted really wanted Tad couldn't give him. Ted fell in love with Tad's ex-wife Dixie. When Tad and Dixie made plans to marry, Ted decided to do in his look-alike during a hunting trip in the Canadian wilderness and take over his life. Before Ted's plan could go into effect, Dixie arrived and Ted disappeared into the woods.

During the holiday season of 1996, Myrtle Fargate (Eileen Herlie) fell in love with Santa Claus (Clifton James) himself, who had taken a room in her boardinghouse. The romance ended with a Christmas Eve face-off between Myrtle and Mrs. Claus, who was also played by Herlie.

Walt Willey and William Christian started off their careers on *All My Children* as extras. Christian played a wrestling teammate of Bob Georgia (Peter Strong). Willey's first professional acting job was playing a barroom patron at Foxy's. He has also played a pilot and Palmer Cortlandt's chauffeur. James Kiberd had also worked on *All My Children* as a day player in the late '70s and early '80s, working in a couple of scenes opposite Taylor Miller (*Nina Cortlandt*).

Donna Pescow, who would take on the role of lesbian doctor Lynn Carson, had an interesting job for *All My Children* in the '70s. She would provide the back of the head that would be seen in audition tapes. Among the actors in whose audition tapes her head appeared was Peter Bergman, who was involved in Lynn's plotline.

Actors Behind the Camera

Agnes Nixon at one time planned to pursue a career in acting. While in college, she realized that her greater talent lay in writing. Like Nixon, many of the creative people behind the camera—the writers, producers, and directors— have worked at one time or another as actors, several of them on the soaps.

Francesca James has worked on *All My Children* in a number of roles and jobs. From 1972 till 1977, she played the fragile dance instructor Kitty Shea. After Kitty died, James left and returned as Kitty's long-lost twin sister Kelly Cole. James left the show again in 1980 and returned to work behind the scenes as a director. Her performance as the drug-addicted singer Kelly Cole won her a Best Supporting Actress Emmy. Her work as a director earned her a handful of Emmy nominations. While working as a director, James would occasionally step in front of the cameras as Kelly, usually for the Christmas episode. James eventually left *All My Children* and headed west. There, she directed and produced a number of soaps, among them

Gillian Spencer (pictured here with James Mitchell) has been nominated for an Emmy as both an actress and a writer. Cathy Blaivas/1984.

Santa Barbara and *General Hospital.* In 1996, she returned to *All My Children* as its executive producer and earned an Emmy nomination in yet another category, Outstanding Daytime Drama.

Gillian Spencer is one of a very select group of day-timers to be nominated for Emmys in both the acting and writing categories. She received her first nomination in 1976 as part of the writing team at *As the World Turns.* She had been given the writing assignment there shortly after her character, Jennifer Hughes, was killed in a car accident. In the 1980s, she managed to balance her role as Daisy Cortlandt on *All My Children* with her duties as co–head writer of the NBC soap *Another World*. Eventually, Spencer cut back on her acting. Daisy visits Pine Valley every so often. Spencer has, however, written for the show and won an Emmy as part of its writing team. She is currently writing for *Another World*.

Courtney Sherman Simon, who has recurred on *All My Children* for several years as psychiatrist Anna Toland, has finally joined the show as a writer. Over the years, she has written for a number of soaps, among them *Guiding Light*. Occasionally, when the need arises for an on-screen psychiatrist, Sherman will step in front of the cameras. She writes under the name Courtney Simon and acts under the name Courtney Sherman.

Before becoming a writer for *All My Children*, the late Clarice Blackburn acted on *Dark Shadows*, *The Doctors*, *Where the Heart Is*, and *As the World Turns*.

All My Children head writer Megan McTavish played Lola Fontaine on *Guiding Light* in the mid-'80s before joining the writing staff.

Before becoming a director, Christopher Goutman acted on *Search for Tomorrow* and *Texas*.

For roughly twenty years, Mary K. Wells worked as an actress on soaps before joining the writing team at *All My Children*. Among the shows she acted on were *Love of Life*, *The Secret Storm*, *Return to Peyton Place*, and *As the World Turns*. She also spent nearly the entire 1960s playing Louise Grimsley Capice on *The Edge of Night*, the on-screen wife to Ray MacDonnell's Phil Capice.

The Artists Formerly Known As . . .

James Patrick Stuart went by his middle name when he joined the cast as Will Cortlandt because the name James Stuart might have gotten him confused with the late screen legend Jimmy Stewart. Unfortunately the name Patrick Stuart ended up getting him confused with Patrick Stewart, who played Captain Picard on *Star Trek: The Next Generation*. Stuart's agent was once contacted by *TV Guide*, who wanted to hire the *Star Trek* Patrick Stewart for a voice-over. When Stuart returned for a brief run to *All My Children* in 1993, he went by his full name, James Patrick Stuart.

When Cady McClain (*Dixie Cooney*) worked in the Peter O'Toole film *My Favorite Year*, she used the more common spelling of her first name, Katie.

Eileen Herlie (*Myrtle Fargate*) dropped a syllable from her family name, Herlihie.

Brian Green, who took over the role of Brian Bodine from Matt Borlenghi, had to add the middle initial L. to his name so as not to be confused with the Brian Green who

Rosa Nevin, née Langshwadt (*Cecily Davidson*), and Mauricio Morales, better known as Maurice Benard (*Nico Kelly*). 1989/Ann Limongello

starred on *Knots Landing*. That other Brian Green now stars on *Beverly Hills 90210* under the name Brian Austin Green. Brian L. Green has also acted under his full name, Brian Lane Green.

John Danelle (*Dr. Frank Grant*) couldn't use his real last name because there was already a John McDonald in the actors union.

Larkin Malloy (*Travis Montgomery*) dropped his given first name, Thomas.

Dack Rambo (*Steve Jacobi*) was born Norman Rambo. His twin brother Dirk was born Orman.

Hunter Tylo, who plays psychiatrist Taylor Hayes on *The Bold and the Beautiful*, went by the name Deborah Morehart when she played Robin McCall on *All My Children*. After marrying Michael Tylo, she not only took his last name, she also decided to use her family name Hunter as a first name.

Maurice Benard (*Nico Kelly*) anglicized his stage name because he found that his birth name, Mauricio Morales, was causing him to be typecast. Benard was his grandmother's maiden name.

Rosa Nevin (*Cecily Davidson*) took her husband's last name, in part because people found her maiden name, Langshwadt, too difficult to pronounce.

Darlene Dahl (*Anita Santos*) also found that people had difficulty pronouncing her last name, Tejeiro. She chose not to wait until she got married to change it. She chose Dahl in honor of her favorite author, Roald Dahl (*Charlie and the Chocolate Factory*).

Relatively Speaking

David Canary, who plays twins Adam and Stuart Chandler, got to work on the show with his real-life brother, John Canary. John played Dr. Voigt, the doctor who sexually harassed intern Angie Hubbard. Although their story lines were for the most part kept separate, the writers did give the brothers Canary a scene together. Dr. Voigt warned Adam that his (Voigt's) wife and Adam's nephew Ross were planning to take over his company.

David Canary and his brother John are descended from legendary cowgirl Calamity Jane, whose real name was Martha Jane Canary.

Like Phoebe Tyler Wallingford, Ruth Warrick can trace her lineage all the way back to the *Mayflower*. Among her ancestors Warrick counts legendary frontiersman Daniel Boone.

Canadian-born Andrew Jackson (*Dr. Stephen Hammill*) is descended from the United States president Andrew Jackson.

Agnes Nixon's oldest daughter, Cathy Chicos, wrote dialogue for the show for several years during the late '70s and early '80s.

Kate Collins, who originated the roles of Natalie Hunter and Janet "from another planet" Green, is the daughter of astronaut Michael Collins, who piloted Apollo 11 on its historic journey to the moon in 1969. While guest-hosting *Good Morning America*, Kate Collins interviewed her father about what it was like walking on the moon.

James Patrick Stuart (*Will Cortlandt*) is the son of Chad Stuart, half of the British folk-rock duo Chad and Jeremy, who recorded hits such as "A Summer Song" in the 1960s.

The late Frances Heflin's (*Mona Kane*) brother Van Heflin acted in a number of radio soaps before making such films such as *Shane*, *Madame Bovary*, and *The Three Musketeers*. In 1942, he won an Academy Award as Best Supporting Actor for his work in *Johnny Eager*. Frances Heflin's children have also pursued careers in show business both in front of the camera and behind it. Her son, Jonathan Kaplan, has directed such feature films as *The Accused* and *Unlawful Entry*. Frances Heflin made a cameo appearance in one of his early films, *Mr. Billions*. Frances Heflin's daughters, Nora Heflin and Mady Kaplan, have had small roles in a number of films directed by their brother. Mady Kaplan, who was also seen in *The Deer Hunter* and *Heaven's Gate*, played Marie Kovac on *As the World Turns*, Margaret Ellington on *Texas*, and District Attorney Lisa Dravicky on *Guiding Light*.

Anne Meara's (*Peggy Moody*) son, Ben Stiller, is a jack-of-all-trades in the entertainment world: actor, writer, director, and producer. He starred in and wrote his own comedy series, *The Ben Stiller Show*. He made his directorial debut with the Wynona Ryder film *Reality Bites*, which he also starred in, and was recently seen in the big-screen comedy *Flirting with Disaster*.

The role of Charlie Brent, son of Tara Martin and Phil Brent, was originated by Ian Washam, whose father was head writer Wisner Washam and whose mother, Judith Barcroft, played Charlie's aunt, Anne Tyler, for several years.

Christopher Lawford, the last actor to play Charlie Brent, is a member of the Kennedy family. His father, British actor Peter Lawford (*Easter Parade*, *Exodus*), married John F. Kennedy's sister Patricia in 1954.

Robert LuPone (*Zach Grayson*) is the brother of TV (*Life Goes On*) and Broadway (*Evita*) star Patti LuPone.

Sydney Penny (*Julia Santos*) is married to Rob Powers, which makes her a great-niece by marriage to longtime *As the World Turns* star Helen Wagner.

Ruth Warrick was once cousin by marriage to Mimi Kennedy, who has written for *Knots Landing* and starred on such prime-time serials as *Homefront* and *Savannah*. Kennedy, who was eight when she first met Warrick, credits her as a major inspiration. In her autobiography *Taken to the Stage: The Education of an Actress*, Kennedy writes of meeting Warrick: "I resolved that I too would be that most glamorous of creatures—an actress!" Warrick later helped Kennedy along in her career by introducing her to the producer of *All My Children*, who in turn helped her land her first exposure on national television as one of the professional liars on the game show *To Tell the Truth*.

Shirley Simmons and Barbara Martin Simmons, who work on *All My Children* as associate directors, are sisters-in-law.

Matt Borlenghi's (*Brian Bodine*) godfather is famed Italian crooner Jerry Vale.

Kelly Ripa and Mark Consuelos (*Hayley Vaughn* and *Mateo Santos*) picked Consuelos's on-screen sister Eva LaRue Callahan (*Dr. Maria Santos*) to be godmother to their son Michael.

True Romance

Kelly Ripa and Mark Consuelos (*Hayley Vaughn* and *Mateo Santos*) fell in love while playing lovers on *All My Children* but kept their relationship secret for a long time. Even after they eloped to Las Vegas, they didn't let the press or their families know that they had gotten married. The pair wanted to tell their families about the wedding in person. When then producer Francesca James discovered that the tabloid press had gotten wind of their secret wedding, she sent both Ripa and Consuelos to their dressing rooms to call their parents and tell them.

Eva LaRue (*Dr. Maria Santos*) was originally brought on as a love interest for Trevor Dillon (James Kiberd). The writers only built the Edmund and Maria romance after they noticed the on-screen chemistry between LaRue and John Callahan (*Edmund Grey*). That on-screen chemistry reflected a real-life romance brewing between the two stars, who married in 1996. They had to cancel the first wedding they planned because the media got wind of it. Their sec-

Edmund Grey (John Callahan) and Dr. Maria Santos (Eva LaRue) married in real life and on-screen. 1994/Ann Limongello

ond and successful attempt took place in Hawaii in front of a small group of family and friends, none of whom were told where the ceremony would take place until a couple of days before. Sarah Michelle Gellar, who had played Kendall Hart on the show, was the only *All My Children* cast member in attendance at the wedding.

One of *All My Children*'s first on-screen couples to become a real-life couple was Charles Frank and Susan

Blanchard, who played Jeff Martin and Mary Kennicott. Frank and Blanchard left the show together in 1975. While Mary was killed off, the role of Jeff was recast.

James Kiberd (*Trevor Dillon*) met his wife Susan Keith while they were playing lovers on *Loving*. When Keith originally auditioned for the role of Shana Alden, Kiberd had told the producers not to hire her.

Emmy winner Mary Fickett (*Ruth Martin*) has long been married to Allen Fristoe, who won an Emmy as a *One Life to Live* director.

Candice Earley (*Donna Tyler*) once dated Clint Ritchie (Clint Buchanan, *One Life to Live*). She is currently married to an Arkansas businessman whom she met on Christmas Day in 1982 when his daughter, a fan of the show, approached Earley on a plane to ask for an autograph. Earley eventually left the show to get married.

Kim Delaney (*Jenny Gardner*) was once married to Charles Grant, who played Preacher Emerson on *The Edge of Night* and now plays Grant Chambers on *The Bold and the Beautiful*.

Michael Sabatino (*Dr. Jonathan Kinder*) fell in love with Crystal Chappell (Maggie Carpenter, *One Life to Live*) while they worked together on *Days of Our Lives*. After leaving the Los Angeles–produced *Days*, the two migrated to East Coast soaps. Sabatino and Chappel married in early 1997 at City Hall in New York.

The roles of Dr. Frank Grant and Nancy Grant were played by John Danelle and Lisa Wilkinson, who had been married to each other in real life before coming on the show. Although the marriage didn't work out, Danelle and Wilkinson continued to play a happily married couple until Frank was killed off in the early '80s.

Dorothy Lyman (*Opal Gardner*) is married to movie producer Vincent Malle (*Alamo Bay*), the brother of the late movie director Louis Malle (*My Dinner with Andre, Au Revoir les Enfants*). In recent years, Lyman herself has been working behind the cameras as a director. Lyman had previously been married to Broadway director John Tillinger.

Ellen Shepherd and Nick Davis were never involved romantically on-screen, but Kathleen Noone dated Larry Keith for ten years. Although they no longer date, the two have remained the best of friends.

Director Christopher Goutman is married to Marcia McCabe, who had a short-term role on *All My Children* as Adam Chandler's lawyer Leslie Duprés. Goutman and McCabe met when they were acting together on *Search for Tomorrow*.

Writer-actress Courtney Sherman (*Dr. Anne Tolen*) also met her husband, actor Peter Simon, while working with him on *Search for Tomorrow*. Peter Simon is best known to soap audiences as Dr. Ed Bauer on *Guiding Light*, where Sherman has also worked as a writer. Her first day of work on *Guiding Light* coincided with the death of her husband's on-screen wife.

Michael E. Knight (*Tad Martin*) is married to Catherine Hickland, who played Julie Clegg on *Capitol* and Tess Wilder on *Loving/The City*. The two met at her birthday party and developed a friendship while taking the same acting class. Prior to Knight, Hickland had been married to David Hasselhoff, who played a character named Michael Knight in his 1980s TV series *Knight Rider*. Early in his career, Knight would often receive fan letters intended for David Hasselhoff, asking about his talking car.

All My Children head writer Wisner Washam is married

to Judith Barcroft, who played Anne Tyler on the show for most of the '70s. Barcroft met Washam while acting on Broadway in *Plaza Suite*. He was the stage manager.

Hunter Tylo (Dr. Taylor Forrester, *The Bold and the Beautiful*) met her husband Michael Tylo (Quint Chamberlain, *Guiding Light*) when they were working on *All My Children* together. Hunter Tylo was playing Robin McCall; Michael Tylo was playing Matt Connolly.

Maxwell Caulfield (*Pierce Riley*) has been married for sixteen years to actress Juliet Mills, best remembered for her work in the 1960s sitcom *Nanny and the Professor*. Mills herself has worked on *All My Children*, playing a judge.

Early in his days on *All My Children*, Peter Bergman (*Cliff Warner*) was married to future film and TV actress Christine Ebersole, who at the time was working on soaps *Ryan's Hope* and *One Life to Live*. Bergman was introduced to his current wife, Mari Ellen, by his former castmate Michael Minor (*Brandon Kingsley*).

Another World star Tom Eplin has been married to two *All My Children* actresses. Ellen Wheeler, who played Cindy Chandler, fell in love with Eplin while they were working together on *Another World*. After their divorce, Eplin married Courtney Eplin, who originated the role of District Attorney Galen Henderson.

Former executive producer Felicia Minei Behr first met her husband Bob Behr during *All My Children*'s early days. She was working as an associate producer on the show, and he as a cameraman.

Anne Meara, who plays Peggy Moody, has long been married to Jerry Stiller, best known for his current role as Frank Costanza on *Seinfeld*. Stiller himself has guest-starred on *All My Children* as a theatrical agent.

Marcy Walker is married to Robert Primrose, a camera technician on the Michael J. Fox sitcom *Spin City*. Walker met Primrose when they were both working on the soap opera *Guiding Light*.

Although Erica Kane has gotten married and divorced some nine times since *All My Children* began, Susan Lucci has been married to only one man, Helmut Huber, for many years. Huber, a former chef, first met Lucci while she was working as a hostess in the hotel restaurant he ran. He ran into her several years later when she was engaged to another man. When things didn't work out between Lucci and her fiancé, Huber began dating her. He asked her to marry him four times before she finally accepted. Huber now works as Lucci's manager.

Agnes Nixon married her late husband, Robert Nixon, after a four-month whirlwind courtship. They were introduced by an older friend of Nixon's, after whom Nixon named the character of Kate Martin. For years, Robert Nixon, who had worked as an executive at Chrysler, served as president of Creative Horizons, which produces *All My Children*.

Matthew Cowles (*Billy Clyde Tuggle*), who has been twice nominated for daytime Emmy awards, is married to Emmy winner Christine Baranski (*Cybil*), who had a small role on *All My Children* as a character named Jewel.

Season Hubley (*Angelique Marrick*) was once married to film star Kurt Russell.

Sandy Gabriel (*Edna Thornton*) has been long been married to John Gabriel, who has worked a number of soaps, most memorably as Dr. Seneca Beaulac on *Ryan's Hope*.

After landing the role of Gloria Marsh, Teresa Blake received a letter from Mike Maguire, the drummer for the country group Shenandoah. Maguire, who had dated Blake when she was in high school, caught her on the show and wrote a letter to congratulate her. The two reconnected, fell back in love, and were eventually married. Among her bridesmaids were Kelly Ripa and Eva LaRue. Blake and Maguire worked together when she played a factory worker in the video for the Shenandoah song "Heaven Bound, I'm Ready."

Distinguished Alumni

Richard Hatch (*Phil Brent*) left *All My Children* just two years into the show's run. He turned up in prime-time as Karl Malden's new partner after Michael Douglas decided to leave the crime drama *The Streets of San Francisco*. From San Francisco, Hatch rocketed into outer space in the science fiction series *Battlestar Galactica*.

Robert Duncan McNeil, who played Phil Brent's son Charlie during the '80s, has landed on a spaceship of his own as the womanizing Lt. Tom Paris on *Star Trek: Voyager*.

Lauren Holly, McNeil's on-screen love interest during his years as Charlie, moved from playing the sweet Julie Chandler to the much tougher police deputy Maxine Stewart in the offbeat drama *Picket Fences*. From there she moved into a steady stream of feature films, ranging from comedies (*Dumb and Dumber*) to thrillers (*Turbulence*).

Two of Erica Kane's daughters have done quite nicely for themselves. Lacey Chabert, who took over the role of Bianca Montgomery for 1993, left for the highly acclaimed

Film star Lauren Holly and *Star Trek: Voyager*'s Robert Duncan McNeil played teen couple Julie and Charlie. 1987/Ann Limongello

Fox drama *Party of Five*, on which she plays an orphaned violinist. Sarah Michelle Gellar, who as Erica's daughter from a rape, Kendall Hart, schemed to make her mother's life hell, is taking on decidedly less dangerous adversaries as the title heroine in the WB horror series *Buffy the Vampire Slayer*. Gellar also popped up on the big screen in Wes Craven's horror sequel *Scream II*.

Kim Delaney's and Melissa Leo's characters were nothing alike on *All My Children*. Delaney's Jenny Gardner

Nanny director Dorothy Lyman and *NYPD Blue*'s Kim Delaney played mother and daughter Opal and Jenny Gardner. 1982/Ann Limongello

was pure and devoted to the equally good Greg Nelson (Laurence Lau), while Leo's Linda Warner, Cliff's (Peter Bergman) younger sister, was drawn to dangerous men. Still, both actresses earned Emmy nominations for their work, and their characters were both killed off by psychopaths whom they'd become involved with. Linda was murdered by her boyfriend Zach Grayson (Robert LuPone), and Jenny was blown up by her ex-fiancé Tony Barclay (Brett Barrett). Leo and Delaney started tracking down murderers and other sordid criminals in two of prime-time's most highly acclaimed police dramas. Melissa Leo played Detective Kay Howard on NBC's *Homicide: Life on the Street* while Delaney recently won an Emmy for playing Detective Diane Russell on ABC's *NYPD Blue*.

Dorothy Lyman impressed *All My Children* fan Carol Burnett so much with her comic turn as Jenny Gardner's tacky mother, Opal, that Burnett hired Lyman to star in the sitcom *Mama's Family*, spun off from a popular sketch on Burnett's old variety series. Lyman juggled both shows for one season, then left *All My Children*. After *Mama's Family* came to an end, Lyman worked briefly on the soaps *Generations* and *The Bold and the Beautiful* and recurred on the prime-time drama *Life Goes On*. There she played the mother of an AIDS-stricken teen, portrayed by Chad Lowe. Charles Frank, who originated the role of Dr. Jeff Martin on *All My Children*, also recurred on the show as the father of a teen with Down's syndrome. Lyman has currently moved back to comedy and behind the camera, directing the Fran Drescher sitcom *The Nanny*.

Eva LaRue Callahan (*Dr. Maria Santos Grey*) has wasted no time in making the transition from daytime to prime-time. She had not even left *All My Children* when it was announced that she would be playing a matchmaker in the UPN sitcom *Head Over Heels*.

For eleven seasons, Amanda Bearse, who played Liza Colby's best friend Amanda Cousins, was seen as the upper-middle-class neighbor Marcy Rhodes Jefferson on Fox's irreverent sitcom *Married . . . with Children*. Also starring on the show was Ed O'Neill, who had a small role as a private investigator on *All My Children* in the early '80s.

O'Neill is but one of the TV and film actors who have passed through Pine Valley on their way to stardom. Oscar winner Kathy Bates (*Misery*) tormented Erica Kane when she was sent to prison after killing Kent Bogard. Oscar nominee Robert Downey Jr. (*Chaplin*) was a member of Pine Valley University's football team. *thirtysomething*'s Timothy Busfield popped up during the crowd scenes on PVU's campus. TV and film star David Allan Grier (*In*

Living Color) chased after Angie Hubbard (Debbi Morgan) as a fellow doctor at the hospital. Playing a patient of Cliff Warner's was Christian Slater (*Heathers*), whose mother was a casting director. The producers were interested in doing more with day player Robert Urich (*Spenser: For Hire, VEGA$*), who landed the work through his brother Tom, also a day player on the show. Robert Urich, however, was concentrating on his theater career at the time.

THE GRADUATES

Match up these actors and actresses currently on other soaps with their roles on *All My Children*. (Answers on page 200)

1. Peter Bergman
   (Jack Abbott, *The Young and the Restless*)

   a. Angie Hubbard

2. Robin Strasser
   (Dorian Lord, *One Life to Live*)

   b. Alec McIntyre

3. Winsor Harmon
   (Thorne Forrester, *The Bold and the Beautiful*)

   c. Ceara Connor

4. Hunter Tylo
   (Dr. Taylor Hayes, *The Bold and the Beautiful*)

   d. Del Henry

5. Charles Keating
   (Carl Hutchins, *Another World*)

   e. Dr. Christina Karras

6. Debbi Morgan
   (Dr. Ellen Burgess, *Port Charles*)

   f. Dr. Cliff Warner

7. Robert Gentry
   (Dr. Ed Bauer, *Guiding Light*)

   g. Robin McCall

8. Genie Francis
   (Laura Spencer, *General Hospital*)

   h. Dr. Damon Lazarre

9. Grant Aleksander
   (Phillip Spaulding, *Guiding Light*)

   i. Ellen Shepherd

10. Kathleen Noone
    (Aunt Bette, *Sunset Beach*)

    j. Ross Chandler

Just Passing Through Town

Carol Burnett has appeared on *All My Children* a number of times over the years. In the '70s, she did a low-key cameo as Mrs. Johnson, a patient being released from Pine Valley Hospital. Joe Martin (Ray MacDonnell) remarked that she looked familiar. Years later, Burnett returned for a week of shows as Verla Grubbs, a carnival friend of Myrtle Fargate's (Eileen Herlie), who discovers that Langley Wallingford (Louis Edmonds) is her biological father. During the show's twenty-fifth-anniversary week, Burnett returned to town as Verla with news that she was getting married. Her fiancé was played by Lucky Vanous, the model-turned-actor famous for his commercial as the Diet Coke–drinking construction worker. Burnett also hosted the ABC prime-time special commemorating *All My Children*'s anniversary.

During Burnett's first appearance as Verla, her good friend Elizabeth Taylor surprised her with a visit. Dressed as a charwoman, Burnett's signature role, Taylor came over and introduced herself to Verla, who was having dinner

Elizabeth Taylor surprised fellow guest Carol Burnett and the audience. (Also pictured is Eileen Herlie as Myrtle Fargate.) 1983/Donna Svennevik

with Myrtle at the Chateau. Burnett was so surprised by Taylor's cameo that she let out an expletive, which forced the scene to be retaped.

As Erica Kane made the transition from small-town girl to high-fashion model, the producers brought on the then top model in the United States, Cheryl Tiegs. Tiegs beat Erica out in a modeling contest, which didn't sit too well with Erica. A fan of the show, Tiegs couldn't wait to come on and put Erica in her place.

Gilligan's Island star Tina Louise played Trish Pridmore, an inmate whom Janet Green ran into while incarcerated for murder. Based on Leona Helmsley, Pridmore was a socialite serving time for tax evasion.

In the early '80s when Kim Fields was starring on *The Facts of Life*, the actress paid a visit to the show as herself. She ran into Cliff Warner (Peter Bergman) while taking a tour of the television station where he hosted a medical show.

All My Children has long been popular with professional athletes, several of whom have appeared on the show. When All My Children traveled to the Superdome in the early '80s, the New Orleans Saints football team turned out in full force to greet Erica Kane. Following the 1988 Superbowl, Erica asked Cincinnati Bengals quarterback Boomer Esiason out on a date to make Travis Montgomery jealous. Erica had also flirted with race car driver Danny Sullivan at a black-tie affair celebrating the Montgomery Cup, an auto race sponsored by Travis's family.

Funnyman Dom DeLuise brought a touch of humor to the story line in which Hayley Vaughn (Kelly Ripa) was kidnapped in the Caribbean. DeLuise, who took the role because so many of his friends are fans of the show, played a traffic cop whom Hayley asks for help while trying to escape her captors.

When the show was looking for a host for its Mrs. Homemaker USA pageant, the producers called upon Bert Parks, who for years had hosted the Miss America pageant.

Comedian, actress, and talk-show host Rosie O'Donnell was originally scheduled to play the photographer shooting Noah Keefer's (Keith Hamilton Cobb) underwear ad but had to cancel that plan because of a personal emergency. She later turned up in Pine Valley as Naomi, filling in for her cousin Winnifred as a maid at the Chandler mansion. A few months later, she returned as Naomi and landed a job at the florist shop on Valentine's Day.

O'Donnell was but the latest in a long line of talk-show hosts who have made their way into Pine Valley. Dick Cavett was the first, playing himself. When he interviewed Erica Kane on his show, she ripped apart the people in

Rosie O'Donnell guest-starred as Adam Chandler's (David Canary) housekeeper Naomi. 1996/Steve Fenn

town. Cavett later returned for the opening of Erica's disco. Virginia Graham, who hosted *Girl Talk* in the '60s, was one of the press people who barged their way into Erica's first wedding to Adam Chandler. Sally Jessy Raphael ran into Adam's brother Stuart Chandler and his fianceé Cindy Parker at the Goalpost while scouting guests for her show. Regis Philbin and Kathie Lee Gifford, along with then Miss America Carolyn Suzanne Sapp, were among the celebrity guests at a fund-raiser Phoebe Tyler Wallingford hosted to benefit the environment. And before she became queen of the talk shows, Oprah Winfrey appeared on *All My Children* as herself, then a Baltimore news anchor. She was in a scene at the New York nightclub Nexus, where she introduced herself to Mark Dalton.

The talk show within the show, *The Cutting Edge*, has allowed for a number of celebrities to play themselves on *All My Children*. Weight-loss guru Richard Simmons, who first came to fame playing himself on *General Hospital*, taught Erica a few new exercises. Cross-dresser, model, and singer RuPaul was also interviewed on *The Cutting Edge* by Erica Kane. When RuPaul landed a talk show on VH1, Susan Lucci was one of the first guests.

When Erica Kane was stuck for a guest while taping the first segment of her talk show, *The Cutting Edge*, her husband Dimitri Marrick (Michael Nader) called on his old friend, singer Aaron Neville. Neville, himself a fan of the show, loved the opportunity to come on and serenade Erica Kane.

While recruiting the legendary Stevie Wonder to perform at a fund-raiser, Erica Kane popped into an impromptu duet of his Oscar-winning single, "I Just Called to Say I Love You," paraphrasing some of the lyrics to plead her case.

Peabo Bryson performed a duet of "Tonight I Celebrate My Love" with Livia Frye (Tonya Pinkins) when she married Tom Cudahy (Richard Shoberg).

After recording the Top 10 single "I Believe," Blessed Union of Souls played the Harvest Dance at Pine Valley High School. To explain why such a popular group would be performing at a high school dance, it was written into the script that the group's manager had graduated from Pine Valley High School.

Erica Kane (Susan Lucci) performed an impromptu duet with guest
Stevie Wonder. 1986/Ann Limongello

The story line in which Mark Dalton (Mark LaMura)
began writing popular music involved two singers. Lesley
Gore, who hit number one in the 1960s with "It's My
Party," played his agent, while singer Melba Moore played
herself and performed Mark's song.

Jimmy Buffett, who had the Top 10 single "Margari-
taville" in the '70s, appeared on *All My Children* but did
not sing. He played a bar patron who talked to Benny Sago
(Vasili Bogazianos) about his gambling habit.

Like Buffett, singer-songwriter Paul Anka ("Put Your
Head on My Shoulder," "You're Having My Baby") was
a fan of the show but did not sing during his appearance
on it. He played himself, introduced as the owner of Nexus.
That scene at Nexus also included mogul Donald Trump,
who rushed onto the *All My Children* set to tape his scene
and then rushed out again.

At the same time that *Raising Kane* was released, New York City mayor Ed Koch had published his own autobiography, *Mayor*. While in New York on business, Erica ran into Koch and compared notes on what it was like to be a best-selling author.

The story line in which Travis Montgomery and his ex-wife Barbara (Susan Pratt) conceive a child together as a possible bone marrow donor for their leukemia-stricken daughter brought then first lady Barbara Bush onto the show. Mrs. Bush taped a message encouraging viewers to sign up with National Registration for bone marrow donors.

More recently, former first lady Betty Ford taped a public service announcement about drug and alcohol addiction. Mrs. Ford's message was repeated several times at the end of episodes in which Erica Kane, who'd become hooked on painkillers, checked into the Betty Ford Clinic.

Famous Fans of the Show

While Walt Willey was attending the Kentucky Derby, a voice called "Jackson" over in his direction. Willey turned around and was surprised to see that the man calling him by his character name was none other than former president George Bush.

Former president Jimmy Carter also had a passing knowledge of the show. His mother, Miss Lillian, was a devoted fan. At one point, she befriended the politically active Ruth Warrick (*Phoebe Tyler*). After watching an episode of *All My Children* with his mother, President Carter described Phoebe Tyler as "the meanest woman I've ever seen."

Carol Burnett remains one of the most famous fans that *All My Children* has and one of its best publicists. During the opening segment of her Saturday night variety series, she would occasionally recap major plot events from the soap. During one such opening segment, she was thrilled to find Nick Benedict (*Phil Brent*) in the audience and pulled him up onstage. While on vacation in Europe before the advent of the VCR, Burnett would be updated with plot synopses via telegram.

While Carol Burnett was the most vocal soap fan, the late Sammy Davis Jr. was one of the first male celebrities to admit that he watched the afternoon soaps. In fact, he planned his whole day around watching his favorite soaps. Although he acted on *One Life to Live* and *General Hospital*, he never made it onto *All My Children*. Once, when he spotted Nick Benedict in traffic, he pulled up beside his car to warn "Phil" not to marry Erica.

Superstar film comic Jim Carrey (*Liar, Liar*; *Ace Ventura*) first caught sight of his then bride-to-be Lauren Holly (*Julie Chandler*) when, in the 1980s, as an out-of-work actor, he followed *All My Children*.

When Ruth Warrick was honored with the Governor's Award for Art Patronage in 1997, screen legend Douglas Fairbanks Jr., with whom she starred in *The Corsican Brothers*, said of her: "If any of you haven't seen her in her daytime television drama, *All My Children*, you probably don't have a television set."

Famed actor-director-producer Orson Welles, who hired Warrick to play his wife in *Citizen Kane*, remained a fan as she moved into television. His blurb on the back of her autobiography read: "The best acting on TV is on daytime serials."

During the '70s, former *Laugh-In* comedian Jo Anne Worley guested on a number of celebrity game shows. As such, when she was home during the day she would leave the TV on to listen to these shows. Because ABC had the most game shows, her TV was usually tuned to her ABC affiliate. As time passed, she grew more and more interested in the soap operas that comprised the majority of the network's afternoon lineup.

Oscar winner Louis Gossett Jr. (*An Officer and a Gentleman*) went over to James Kiberd and his wife Susan Keith during a parade to let them know how much he and his wife enjoyed watching both *Loving* and *All My Children*.

Country music star Reba McEntire has been watching the ABC soaps since she was a girl. In the spring of 1997, she not only hosted *A Daytime to Remember*, which rebroadcast classic episodes of *All My Children*, she also introduced the clip package from *All My Children* at the 1997 Daytime Emmy Awards.

Sarah Michelle Gellar and Eva LaRue were excited to watch the 1960s girl group The Marvelettes perform at a benefit for the Starlight Foundation. The Marvelettes, who recorded the number one single "Please Mr. Postman," were equally thrilled to find "Kendall and Maria" in the audience.

Calvert DeForest, better known to David Letterman fans as Larry "Bud" Melman, once told Michael E. Knight that he counts among his favorite soap scenes the one in which Tad was blown off the bridge by Billy Clyde Tuggle.

Talk show host Rolanda Watts has been watching *All My Children* since she was thirteen years old. As such, she was thrilled the first time she got to interview Susan Lucci.

Dorien Wilson, who co-starred on the HBO sitcom *Dream On*, was more than a little familiar with the work of Vanessa Bell Calloway, who played his wife for several episodes on the series. He remembered her from her days as Yvonne Caldwell on *All My Children*, which he has been following since the early '80s.

Actress Virginia Madsen (*Candyman, Slamdance*), who has a child with former *General Hospital* star Antonio Sabato Jr., told Brian Gaskill (*Bobby Warner*) that she loves *All My Children*.

While on *Oprah* to promote *Soapdish*, the comedy in which she played a soap opera actress, the Oscar-nomated actress Elisabeth Shue (*Leaving Las Vegas*) admitted that she was hooked on *All My Children* as a teen.

Like Shue, Oprah Winfrey is a longtime fan of *All My Children*. She has featured actors from the soap on her talk show a number of times and on one memorable episode, reunited Susan Lucci with almost all her former leading men.

When *Blossom* star Mayim Bialik met Ruth Warrick at a charity function, she wanted an update on what was happening in Pine Valley.

Richard Roundtree, who made a name for himself playing private investigator Shaft in films and on television, used to watch *All My Children* in his trailer during lunch breaks. He was such a fan that he once went running after Darnell Williams (*Jesse Hubbard*) and Kim Delaney (*Jenny Gardner*) when he saw them pass by the window of the restaurant where he was dining.

Kate Pierson of the alternative rock group the B-52s ("Private Idaho," "Rock Lobster") first started watching *All My Children* while working with audiovisual equipment at the Georgia Center for Continuing Education. One of the men she worked with who watched *All My Children* would turn on the soap under the pretense that something should be on the monitors. Little by little, Pierson became a fan. Even her cat got hooked on the show and perked up every time Eileen Herlie (*Myrtle Fargate*), a redhead like Pierson, came on-screen. Pierson took it as "the ultimate compliment" when the B-52s' "Love Shack" was playing in the background during a scene on the show.

Like Kate Pierson, soul singer–songwriter Luther Vandross ("Love Power") loves to hear his songs played in
the background on *All My Children*. His interest in the
show goes all the way back to his days as a studio singer.

At a charity event, pop diva Whitney Houston walked
up to a group of actors from *All My Children*—among them
Ruth Warrick, Julia Barr, and John Callahan—to let them
know she knew who they were because she watched the
show.

Tennis player Zina Garrison used to make fun of her
mother and sisters for watching *All My Children* every day.
Then her career got temporarily derailed by health problems. During her time away from tennis, Garrison got
hooked on *All My Children*. Fellow tennis player Gabriela
Sabatini introduced Garrison to Dondre T. Whitfeld (*Terrence Frye*), who gave them a tour of the *All My Children*
set.

Garrison is far from the only *All My Children* fan on
the tennis circuit. Susan Lucci learned while attending a
tournament in the Bahamas that Billie Jean King and Chris
Evert preferred not to play any matches at one o'clock if
they could help it.

Baseball player Dave Cone of the New York Yankees
prides himself on the fact that he can remember all the way
back to Erica's first marriage to Jeff Martin.

Professional basketball star Charles Barkley once
showed up late for an afternoon game because he was
watching the end of *All My Children*.

Screen legend Elizabeth Taylor got hooked on the ABC
afternoon lineup while she was living in Washington, D.C.,
as the wife of Senator John Warner.

Rosie O'Donnell specifically requested that Susan

Lucci be a guest on the first day of her talk show. She has since had a number of Lucci's castmates on her program.

Other fans of *All My Children* include actor Mike Myers (*Wayne's World*, *Austin Powers*), singer Gladys Knight, actress Rosie Perez (*Fearless*, *White Men Can't Jump*), Judy Garland's daughter actress-singer Lorna Luft, and Nichelle Nichols, who played Lieutenant Uhura on the original *Star Trek* series.

Cast Members Who Were Fans First

Michael E. Knight (*Tad Martin*) first checked out *All My Children* when he was in his early teens. He was laid up in bed for a week with a broken arm and a sprained ankle. At the time, his future on-screen sister Tara was searching for an amnesiac Phil Brent. That one week was enough for Knight to get the feeling for what it was like to live in Pine Valley.

Darlene Dahl (*Anita Santos*) has been watching *All My Children* since she was eight years old. It was one of the reasons she became interested in acting.

Tonya Pinkins (*Livia Frye*), who has been watching *All My Children* since she was eight, remained a fan even while working as Heather Dalton on *As the World Turns*. Of course, the role she had really wanted was that of Angie Baxter, which she auditioned for when it was first introduced.

Like Dahl and Pinkins, Ingrid Rodgers (*Taylor Roxbury Cannon*) had been tuning in to the show since she was a child. Among her all-time favorite couples was Angie and Jesse.

Tad "the Cad" Martin and his southern belle Dixie (Michael E. Knight and Cady McClain). 1993/E. J. Carr

Mark Consuelos, who was born in Spain, learned how to speak English in part by watching American soap operas, like *All My Children*, with his family.

Lauren Roman (*Laura Kirk*) believes that she has been preparing for her role since before she was born. Her mother, a devoted fan of the show, watched while she was pregnant with Lauren, who inherited her mother's love for Pine Valley at a very early age.

Winsor Harmon was a devoted fan of *All My Children* in high school. He watched every day and taped the show during the summer months. His role as Del Henry gave him a chance to work with a number of his favorite actors on the show, including Susan Lucci and James Mitchell.

Harmon's on-screen father Steve Kanaly (*Seabone Hunkle*) also had long been following the show, mainly because his wife was such a fan. When he was offered the role of Seabone, his wife did not give him a chance to turn it down.

Leslie Uggams and her whole family have been long-time fans of the show. Her family was more excited about her landing the role of Noah Keefer's (Keith Hamilton Cobb) mother Rose than about anything else she's ever done in her film, music, theater, and TV career.

Daytime Emmy Curiosities

Soap operas have been airing on television since the late '40s, but outside of a few half-hearted nominations in the '60s, the Emmy awards did not recognize soaps until 1972, when *The Doctors* won the award for Outstanding Achievement in Daytime Drama. The following year, *All My Children*'s Mary Fickett (*Ruth Martin*) won the first Emmy awarded to a performer. Her category, Outstanding Achievement by an Individual in Daytime Drama, had Fickett competing against Macdonald Carey from *Days of Our Lives*, three directors, a scenic designer, and a set decorator. By the following year, the Daytime Emmys had broken off into their own ceremony, which separated actors from actresses and performers from behind-the-scenes personnel. Still, the Daytime Emmys have included their fair share of oddities and curiosities.

Susan Lucci (*Erica Kane*) holds the record for racking up the most acting nominations—seventeen—without winning the award. Those seventeen nominations also give

Lucci the overall record for most acting nominations in the Daytime Emmys.

The actor who has racked up the most nominations without winning is Lucci's castmate James Mitchell, who has been nominated seven times in both the Best Actor and Best Supporting Actor categories for his performance as Palmer Cortlandt.

All My Children itself was nominated for Outstanding Daytime Drama fifteen times before it finally won. Agnes Nixon was nominated nine times for her writing before she won.

The only tie in the writing category occurred in 1997 when *All My Children* tied with *The Young and the Restless*.

The only tie in a soap opera acting category happened in 1989 when Debbi Morgan (*Dr. Angie Hubbard*) tied for Best Supporting Actress with *Santa Barbara*'s Nancy Grahn.

The only time that three actors from the same show were nominated for Best Actor occurred in 1985. Darnell Williams, James Mitchell, and David Canary were each nominated; Williams won.

The only other Emmy *All My Children* had to share was the 1990 Emmy for Costume Design. *All My Children* tied with *Another World*.

Francesca James is the only daytimer to be nominated as a performer, director, and producer for the same show. She won the 1980 Emmy as Best Supporting Actress for her work as Kelly Cole. Several times during the 1980s, she was nominated as part of the show's directing team. And in 1997, after winning an Emmy as one of the producers on *General Hospital*, she was up for an Emmy for her work as executive producer of *All My Children*.

Debbi Morgan tied for the Best Supporting Actress Emmy in 1989. 1989/
Steve Fenn

Gillian Spencer is one of only a handful of performers
who has been nominated for both acting and writing Emmys. She was nominated for her first Emmy as a writer on
As the World Turns in the mid-'70s. During the mid-'80s,
she was nominated as Best Actress for her work as Daisy
Cortlandt on *All My Children* and later won an Emmy as
part of the show's writing team.

Opal Gardner is one of the few roles on daytime television that have earned Emmy nominations for different

Adam Chandler's masquerade ball. 1989/Ann Limongello

performers. Dorothy Lyman won two Emmys as Opal, and Jill Larson has been Emmy nominated twice for her work as Opal.

Dorothy Lyman is also one of the few performers who has won a Daytime Emmy as Supporting Actress and Lead Actress. Darnell Williams (*Jesse Hubbard*) has similarly won Emmys as supporting and then lead actor.

Lynne Thigpen has never entered her name into consideration for an Emmy for her work on *All My Children* but has been nominated several times for her work on the children's game show *Where in the World Is Carmen Sandiego?*

Singer–songwriter Peabo Bryson won an Emmy for the song he penned as Erica and Dimitri's theme, "I Found Love."

Susan Lucci has co-hosted the Emmys four times: in 1991 with talk show host Phil Donahue; in 1992 with for-

mer leading man Walt Willey; in 1993 with ex–Cliff Warner Peter Bergman (Jack Abbott, *The Young and the
Restless*), Drake Hogestyn (John Black, *Days of Our Lives*),
and James DePaiva (Max Holden, *One Life to Live*), and
in 1997 with talk-show host Regis Philbin.

All My Children's Emmy Winners and Nominees

1973 EMMY AWARDS

Outstanding Achievement by an Individual in Daytime Drama: Mary Fickett (*Ruth Martin*)

1974 DAYTIME EMMY AWARDS

Best Actress nominee: Mary Fickett (*Ruth Martin*)

1975 DAYTIME EMMY AWARDS

Best Actress nominee: Ruth Warrick (*Phoebe Tyler*)

1976 DAYTIME EMMY AWARDS

Outstanding Daytime Drama Series nominee: *All My Children* (Bud Kloss, producer)

Outstanding Actress nominee: Frances Heflin (*Mona Kane*)

Outstanding Writing nominee: *All My Children* (Agnes Nixon, head writer)

1977 DAYTIME EMMY AWARDS

Outstanding Daytime Drama nominee: *All My Children* (Bud Kloss and Agnes Nixon, producers)

Outstanding Actor nominee: Lawrence Keith (*Nick Davis*)

Outstanding Actress nominee: Ruth Warrick (*Phoebe Tyler*)

Outstanding Writing nominee: *All My Children* (Agnes Nixon, Wisner Washam, Kathryn McCabe, Mary K. Wells, and Jack Wood)

1978 DAYTIME EMMY AWARDS

Outstanding Daytime Series nominees: *All My Children* (Bud Kloss and Agnes Nixon, producers)

Outstanding Actor nominees: Matthew Cowles (*Billy Clyde Tuggle*) and Larry Keith (*Nick Davis*)

Outstanding Actress nominees: Mary Fickett (*Ruth Martin*) and Susan Lucci (*Erica Kane*)

Outstanding Writing nominee: *All My Children* (Agnes Nixon, Wisner Washam, Cathy Chicos, Doris Frankel, Ken Harvey, Mary K. Wells, Kathryn McCabe, and Jack Wood)

1979 Daytime Emmy Awards

Outstanding Daytime Drama nominee: *All My Children* (Agnes Nixon, executive producer; Bud Kloss, producer)
Outstanding Actor nominee: Nicholas Benedict (*Phil Brent*)
Outstanding Direction nominee: *All My Children* (Jack Coffey, Del Hughes, and Henry Kaplan)
Outstanding Writing nominee: *All My Children* (Agnes Nixon, Wisner Washam, Jack Wood, Mary K. Wells, Cathy Chicos, Caroline Franz, Doris Frankel, and William Delligan)

1980 Daytime Emmy Awards

Outstanding Supporting Actor: Warren Burton (*Eddie Dorrance*)
Outstanding Supporting Actress: Francesca James (*Kelly Cole*)
Outstanding Technical Excellence: *All My Children*
Outstanding Design Excellence: *All My Children*
Outstanding Daytime Drama Series nominee: *All My Children* (Agnes Nixon, executive producer; Jorn Winther, producer)
Outstanding Actor nominees: James Mitchell (*Palmer Cortlandt*) and William Mooney (*Paul Martin*)
Outstanding Actress nominees: Julia Barr (*Brooke English*) and Kathleen Noone (*Ellen Shepherd*)
Outstanding Cameo Appearance nominee: Eli Mintz (*the locksmith*)
Outstanding Direction nominee: *All My Children* (Henry

Kaplan, Jack Coffey, Sherrell Hoffman, and Jorn Winther)

Outstanding Writing nominee: *All My Children* (Agnes Nixon, Wisner Washam, Jack Wood, Mary K. Wells, Cathy Chicos, Caroline Franz, Clarice Blackburn, Anita Jaffe, and Ken Harvey)

1981 DAYTIME EMMY AWARDS

Outstanding Achievement in Technical Excellence: *All My Children*

Outstanding Individual Achievement in Any Area of Creative Technical Crafts (Technical Director/Electronic Camera): *All My Children*

Outstanding Daytime Drama nominee: *All My Children* (Agnes Nixon, executive producer; Jorn Winther, producer)

Outstanding Actor nominee: James Mitchell (*Palmer Cortlandt*)

Outstanding Actress nominees: Julia Barr (*Brooke English*) and Susan Lucci (*Erica Kane*)

Outstanding Supporting Actor nominees: Matthew Cowles (*Billy Clyde Tuggle*) and William Mooney (*Paul Martin*)

Outstanding Direction nominee: *All My Children* (Larry Auerbach, Jack Coffey, Sherrell Hoffman, and Jorn Winther)

Outstanding Writing nominee: *All My Children* (Agnes Nixon, Wisner Washam, Clarice Blackburn, Jack Wood, Mary K. Wells, Cathy Chicos, Caroline Franz, and Cynthia Benjamin)

1982 DAYTIME EMMY AWARDS

Outstanding Supporting Actress: Dorothy Lyman (*Opal Gardner*)

Outstanding Technical Excellence: *All My Children*

Outstanding Individual Achievement in Any Area of Creative Technical Crafts (Electronic Camera): *All My Children*

Outstanding Daytime Drama Series nominee: *All My Children* (Jorn Winther, producer)

Outstanding Actor nominees: James Mitchell (*Palmer Cortlandt*) and Richard Shoberg (*Tom Cudahy*)

Outstanding Actress nominee: Susan Lucci (*Erica Kane*)

Outstanding Supporting Actor nominee: Darnell Williams (*Jesse Hubbard*)

Outstanding Supporting Actress nominee: Elizabeth Lawrence (*Myra Murdoch*)

Outstanding Direction nominee: *All My Children* (Larry Auerbach, Jack Coffey, Sherrell Hoffman, and Jorn Winther)

Outstanding Writing nominee: *All My Children* (Agnes Nixon, Wisner Washam, Clarice Blackburn, Jack Wood, Mary K. Wells, Caroline Franz, Lorraine Broderick, John Saffron, Elizabeth Wallace, and Cynthia Benjamin)

1983 DAYTIME EMMY AWARDS

Outstanding Actress: Dorothy Lyman (*Opal Gardner*)

Outstanding Supporting Actor: Darnell Williams (*Jesse Hubbard*)

Outstanding Technical Excellence: *All My Children*

Outstanding Design Excellence: *All My Children*

Outstanding Daytime Drama nominee: *All My Children* (Jacqueline Babbin, producer)

Outstanding Actor nominees: Peter Bergman (*Dr. Cliff Warner*) and James Mitchell (*Palmer Cortlandt*)

Outstanding Actress nominee: Susan Lucci (*Erica Kane*)

Outstanding Supporting Actress nominees: Kim Delaney (*Jenny Gardner*) and Marcy Walker (*Liza Colby*)

Outstanding Direction nominee: *All My Children* (Larry Auerbach, Jack Coffey, Sherrell Hoffman, and Francesca James)

Outstanding Writing nominee: *All My Children* (Agnes Nixon, Wisner Washam, Clarice Blackburn, Jack Wood, Mary K. Wells, Caroline Franz, Lorraine Broderick, John Saffron, and Elizabeth Wallace)

1984 DAYTIME EMMY AWARDS

Special Classification of Outstanding Individual Achievement (Audio): *All My Children*

Outstanding Daytime Drama Series nominee: *All My Children* (Jacqueline Babbin, producer)

Outstanding Actor nominee: James Mitchell (*Palmer Cortlandt*)

Outstanding Actress nominee: Susan Lucci (*Erica Kane*)

Outstanding Supporting Actor nominee: Louis Edmonds (*Langley Wallingford*)

Outstanding Supporting Actress nominees: Eileen Herlie (*Myrtle Fargate*) and Marcy Walker (*Liza Colby*)

Outstanding Direction nominee: *All My Children* (Jack Coffey, Sherrell Hoffman, Henry Kaplan, and Francesca James)

Outstanding Writing nominee: *All My Children* (Agnes

Nixon, Wisner Washam, Lorraine Broderick, Dani Morris, Clarice Blackburn, Jack Wood, Mary K. Wells, Elizabeth Wallace, Roni Dengel, Susan Kirshenbaum, and Carolina Della Pietra)

1985 DAYTIME EMMY AWARDS

Outstanding Actor: Darnell Williams (*Jesse Hubbard*)

Outstanding Writing: *All My Children* (Agnes Nixon, Wisner Washam, Lorraine Broderick, Victor Miller, Clarice Blackburn, Jack Wood, Mary K. Wells, Art Wallace, Susan Kirshenbaum, Elizabeth Page, and Carolina Della Pietra)

Outstanding Daytime Drama Series nominee: *All My Children* (Jacqueline Babbin, producer)

Outstanding Actor nominees: David Canary (*Adam and Stuart Chandler*) and James Mitchell (*Palmer Cortlandt*)

Outstanding Actress nominees: Susan Lucci (*Erica Kane*) and Gillian Spencer (*Daisy Cortlandt*)

Outstanding Supporting Actor nominees: Louis Edmonds (*Langley Wallingford*) and Robert LuPone (*Zach Grayson*)

Outstanding Supporting Actress nominees: Eileen Herlie (*Myrtle Fargate*) and Elizabeth Lawrence (*Myra Murdoch*)

Outstanding Juvenile/Young Man nominees: Steve Caffrey (*Andrew Preston*) and Michael E. Knight (*Tad Martin*)

Outstanding Ingenue nominees: Melissa Leo (*Linda Warner*) and Tasia Valenza (*Dottie Thorton*)

Outstanding Direction nominees: *All My Children* (Jack Coffey, Sherrell Hoffman, Henry Kaplan, Francesca

James, Jean Dadario Burke, and Barbara Martin Simmons)

1986 DAYTIME EMMY AWARDS

Outstanding Actor: David Canary (*Adam and Stuart Chandler*)

Outstanding Younger Leading Man: Michael E. Knight (*Tad Martin*)

Outstanding Daytime Drama nominee: *All My Children* (Jacqueline Babbin, producer)

Outstanding Actress nominee: Susan Lucci (*Erica Kane*)

Oustanding Supporting Actor nominee: Louis Edmonds (*Langley Wallingford*)

Outstanding Supporting Actress nominee: Eileen Herlie (*Myrtle Fargate*)

Outstanding Ingenue nominee: Debbi Morgan (*Angie Hubbard*)

1987 DAYTIME EMMY AWARDS

Outstanding Supporting Actress: Kathleen Noone (*Ellen Shepherd*)

Outstanding Younger Leading Man: Michael E. Knight (*Tad Martin*)

Outstanding Daytime Drama Series nominee: *All My Children* (Jacqueline Babbin and Jorn Winther, producers; Randi Subarsky, coordinating producer)

Outstanding Actress nominee: Susan Lucci (*Erica Kane*)

Outstanding Guest Performer nominee: Pamela Blair (*Ronda*)

Outstanding Direction nominee: *All My Children* (Jack Coffey, Sherrell Hoffman, Henry Kaplan, Francesca James, Jean Dadario Burke, Barbara Martin Simmons, and Shirley Simmons)

1988 DAYTIME EMMY AWARDS

Outstanding Lead Actor: David Canary (*Adam and Stuart Chandler*)

Outstanding Supporting Actress: Ellen Wheeler (*Cindy Parker*)

Outstanding Writing: *All My Children* (Agnes Nixon, Clarice Blackburn, Lorraine Broderick, Susan Kirshenbaum, Kathleen Klein, Karen L. Lewis, Victor Miller, Megan McTavish, Elizabeth Page, Peggy Sloane, Gillian Spencer, Elizabeth Wallace, Wisner Washam, Jack Wood, and Mary K. Wells)

Outstanding Drama Series nominee: *All My Children* (Stephen Schenkel, producer; Thomas de Villiers and Kristen Laskas Martin, coordinating producers)

Outstanding Lead Actor nominee: Robert Gentry (*Ross Chandler*)

Outstanding Lead Actress nominee: Susan Lucci (*Erica Kane*)

Outstanding Supporting Actor nominee: Mark LaMura (*Mark Dalton*)

Outstanding Younger Leading Man nominee: Robert Duncan McNeil (*Charlie Brent*)

Outstanding Ingenue nominee: Lauren Holly (*Julie Chandler*)

1989 DAYTIME EMMY AWARDS

Outstanding Lead Actor: David Canary (*Adam and Stuart Chandler*)

Outstanding Supporting Actress: Debbi Morgan (*Angie Hubbard*) tied with Nancy Lee Grahn (Julia Wainwright, *Santa Barbara*)

Outstanding Lighting Direction: *All My Children*

Outstanding Drama Series nominee: *All My Children* (Stephen Schenkel, producer; Thomas de Villiers and Kristen Laskas Martin, coordinating producers)

Outstanding Lead Actor nominee: James Mitchell (*Palmer Cortlandt*)

Outstanding Lead Actress nominee: Susan Lucci (*Erica Kane*)

1990 DAYTIME EMMY AWARDS

Outstanding Supporting Actress: Julia Barr (*Brooke English*)

Outstanding Juvenile Female: Cady McClain (*Dixie Cooney*)

Outstanding Costume Design: *All My Children* tied with *Another World*

Outstanding Drama Series nominee: *All My Children* (Felicia Minei Behr, executive producer; Thomas de Villiers and Terry Cacavio, coordinating producers)

Oustanding Lead Actor nominee: David Canary (*Adam and Stuart Chandler*)

Outstanding Lead Actress nominee: Susan Lucci (*Erica Kane*)

Outstanding Supporting Actor nominee: Robert Gentry
(*Ross Chandler*)

Outstanding Juvenile Female nominee: Liz Vassey (*Emily
Ann Sago*)

Outstanding Directing Team nominee: *All My Children*
(Jack Coffey, Christopher Goutman, Henry Kaplan,
Conal O'Brien, Barbara Martin Simmons, and Shirley
Simmons)

Outstanding Writing nominee: *All My Children* (Agnes
Nixon, Wisner Washam, Lorraine Broderick, Margaret
DePriest, Susan Kirshenbaum, Kathleen Klein, Karen L.
Lewis, Megan McTavish, Victor Miller, Elizabeth Page,
Elizabeth Smith, Gillian Spencer, and Mary K. Wells)

1991 DAYTIME EMMY AWARDS

Outstanding Drama Series nominee: *All My Children* (Felicia Minei Behr, executive producer; Thomas de Villiers
and Terry Cacavio, coordinating producers)

Oustanding Lead Actor nominee: David Canary (*Adam and
Stuart Chandler*)

Outstanding Lead Actress nominees: Julia Barr (*Brooke English*) and Susan Lucci (*Erica Kane*)

Outstanding Supporting Actor nominee: William Christian
(*Derek Frye*)

Outstanding Supporting Actress nominee: Jill Larson (*Opal
Gardner*)

Outstanding Directing Team nominee: *All My Children*
(Jack Coffey, Christopher Goutman, Henry Kaplan,
Conal O'Brien, Barbara Martin Simmons, and Shirley
Simmons)

Outstanding Writing nominee: *All My Children* (Agnes

Nixon, Wisner Washam, Lorraine Broderick, Susan Kirshenbaum, Kathleen Klein, Karen L. Lewis, Megan McTavish, Michelle Patrick, Elizabeth Smith, Gillian Spencer, and Mary K. Wells)

1992 DAYTIME EMMY AWARDS

Outstanding Drama Series: *All My Children* (Felicia Minei Behr, executive producer; Thomas de Villiers, Terry Cacavio, Nancy Horwich, and Christine Banas, producers)

Outstanding Lead Actor nominee: David Canary (*Adam and Stuart Chandler*)

Outstanding Lead Actress nominee: Susan Lucci (*Erica Kane*)

Outstanding Younger Actor nominees: Patrick Stuart (*Will Cortlandt*) and Dondre Whitfield (*Terrence Frye*)

Outstanding Younger Actress nominee: Cady McClain (*Dixie Cooney*)

Outstanding Writing Team nominee: *All My Children* (Agnes Nixon, Wisner Washam, Lorraine Broderick, Susan Kirshenbaum, Kathleen Klein, Jeff Beldner, Hal Corley, Richard Culliton, Karen L. Lewis, Megan McTavish, Michelle Patrick, Elizabeth Smith, Gillian Spencer, and Mary K. Wells)

1993 DAYTIME EMMY AWARDS

Outstanding Lead Actor: David Canary (*Adam and Stuart Chandler*)

Outstanding Original Song: "I Found Love," by Peabo Bryson (written for *All My Children*)

David Canary has won four Emmys for playing twins Adam and Stuart Chandler. 1986/Ann Limongello

Outstanding Daytime Drama nominee: *All My Children* (Felicia Minei Behr, executive producer; Terry Cacavio, Thomas de Villiers, and Nancy Horwich, producers)

Outstanding Lead Actress nominees: Julia Barr (*Brooke English*) and Susan Lucci (*Erica Kane*)

Outstanding Supporting Actress nominee: Jill Larson (*Opal Gardner Cortlandt*)

Outstanding Younger Actor nominees: Matt Borlenghi (*Brian Bodine*) and Dondre Whitfield (*Terrence Frye*)

Outstanding Directing Team nominee: *All My Children* (Christopher Goutman, Jack Coffey, Henry Kaplan, Conal O'Brien, Barbara Simmons, and Shirley Simmons)

Outstanding Writing Team nominee: *All My Children* (Agnes Nixon, Susan Kirshenbaum, Kathleen Klein, Jeff Beldner, Hal Corley, Richard Culliton, Carolyn Culliton,

Judith Donato, Karen L. Lewis, Megan McTavish, Michelle Patrick, and Elizabeth Smith)

1994 DAYTIME EMMY AWARDS

Outstanding Drama Series: *All My Children* (Felicia Minei Behr, executive producer; Terry Cacavio, Thomas de Villiers, Lisa Hesser, and Nancy Horwich, producers)
Outstanding Lead Actress nominee: Julia Barr (*Brooke English*)
Outstanding Younger Actor nominee: Dondre Whitfield (*Terrence Frye*)
Outstanding Younger Actress nominee: Sarah Michelle Gellar (*Kendall Hart*)
Outstanding Directing Team nominee: *All My Children* (Christopher Goutman, Jack Coffey, Henry Kaplan, Conal O'Brien, Robin Maizes, Barbara Simmons, and Shirley Simmons)

1995 DAYTIME EMMY AWARDS

Outstanding Younger Actress: Sarah Michelle Gellar (*Kendall Hart*)
Outstanding Directing Team: *All My Children* (Christopher Goutman, Henry Kaplan, Conal O'Brien, James Baffico, Sybil Costello, Robin Maizes, Barbara Simmons, and Shirley Simmons)
Outstanding Writing Team nominee: *All My Children* (Agnes Nixon, Megan McTavish, Bettina Bradley, Hal Corley, Frederick Johnson, Gail Lawrence, Karen Lewis,

Michelle Patrick, Pete Rich, Elizabeth Smith, and Ralph
Wakefield)

Outstanding Technical Direction/Electronic Camera/Video
Control: *All My Children*

Outstanding Live and Tape Sound Mixing and Sound Ef-
fects: *All My Children*

Outstanding Daytime Drama nominee: *All My Children*
(Felicia Minei Behr, executive producer; Terry Cacavio,
Lisa Hesser, and Nancy Horwich, producers)

Outstanding Lead Actor nominee: David Canary (*Adam
and Stuart Chandler*)

Outstanding Lead Actress nominee: Susan Lucci (*Erica
Kane*)

Outstanding Supporting Actor nominee: Keith Hamilton
Cobb (*Noah Keefer*)

Outstanding Supporting Actress nominee: Sydney Penny
(*Julia Santos*)

Outstanding Younger Actor nominee: Tommy J. Michaels
(*Timmy Dillon*)

1996 DAYTIME EMMY AWARDS

Outstanding Writing Team: *All My Children* (Agnes Nixon,
Megan McTavish, Lorraine Broderick, Jeff Beldner, Bet-
tina Bradbury, Hal Corley, Judith Donato, Frederick
Johnson, Kathleen Klein, Gail Lawrence, Karen Lewis,
Michelle Patrick, Pete Rich, Elizabeth Smith, and Ralph
Wakefield)

Outstanding Daytime Drama nominee: *All My Children*
(Felicia Minei Behr, executive producer; Terry Cacavio,
Lisa Hesser, Nancy Horwich, and Gary Tomlin, pro-
ducers)

Outstanding Lead Actor nominee: David Canary (*Adam and Stuart Chandler*)

Outstanding Lead Actress nominee: Susan Lucci (*Erica Kane*)

Outstanding Directing Team nominee: *All My Children* (Christopher Goutman, Conal O'Brien, James Baffico, Sybil Costello, Robin Maizes, Henry Kaplan, Barbara Simmons, and Shirley Simmons)

1997 DAYTIME EMMY AWARDS

Outstanding Writing Team (tied): *All My Children* (Agnes Nixon, Lorraine Broderick, Millee Taggart, Hal Corley, Frederick Johnson, Jeff Beldner, Christina Covino, Courtney Simon, Karen Lewis, Elizabeth Smith, Michelle Patrick, Bettina Bradbury, Kathleen Klein, and Jane Owen Murphy) tied with *The Young and the Restless*

Outstanding Drama Series nominee: *All My Children* (Francesca James, executive producer; Linda Barker, producer; Terry Cacavio, supervising producer; Kevin Gill, Nancy Horwich and Lisa S. Hesser, coordinating producers)

Outstanding Lead Actress nominee: Susan Lucci (*Erica Kane*)

Outstanding Lead Actor nominee: David Canary (*Adam and Stuart Chandler*)

Outstanding Supporting Actress nominee: Eva LaRue Callahan (*Dr. Maria Santos*)

Outstanding Directing Team nominee: *All My Children* (Conal O'Brien, James A. Baffico, Henry Kaplan, Jill Ackles, Andrew Lee, Barbara Martin Simmons, and Shirley Simmons)

Literary Merits

All My Children: The Complete Family Scrapbook by Gary Warner landed on *The New York Times* hardcover bestseller list during the winter of 1995, the first soap opera–related book ever to do so. The coffee table–sized book recaps the show's plot history from the very beginning to midway through 1994. Special sections cover the show's most notorious villains, most romantic couples and weddings, and most important families. In addition to hundreds of photographs, the book also includes backstage stories from many of the show's cast members, past and present. This book's success pretty much set the standard for the slew of soap opera anniversary books that followed.

Predating Warner's book by almost twenty years was Dan Wakefield's *All Her Children* (Doubleday & Company, 1976). Author of such best-selling novels as *Starting Over* and *Going All the Way*, Wakefield was a devoted fan of *All My Children*. Early into the show's run, he went backstage to write about it. His effort is one of the very first books devoted to a single daytime soap opera.

Louis Edmonds (*Langley Wallingford*) and Ruth Warrick (*Phoebe Tyler*) each have published their autobiographies. 1989/Ann Limongello

In 1981, Jove Publications issued three paperback novelizations about the denizens of Pine Valley. All three volumes of the series, titled *Agnes Nixon's All My Children*, were written by Rosemarie Santini. She had previously written not only novels but the nonfiction work *The Secret Fire: How Women Live Their Sexual Fantasies.* Volume 1 of her *All My Children* series was subtitled *Tara and Philip*; Volume 2, *Erica*; and Volume 3, *The Lovers.*

In 1980, Ruth Warrick published her autobiography, *The Confessions of Phoebe Tyler.* The book covered her career from her film roles right up through her work on *All My Children.* In addition to recounting Warrick's own life story, the book also took readers behind the scenes at *All My Children* and included capsule biographies of the show's major characters.

Sixteen years after Ruth Warrick published her autobiography, her longtime leading man Louis Edmonds (*Langley Wallingford*) published his own autobiography, which he titled *Big Lou*.

The biography *Susan Lucci: The Woman Behind Erica Kane* (St. Martin's Press, 1986), was written by the husband-and-wife team of Barbara and Scott Siegel. It is dedicated "in memory of Mike Roy," Erica's love interest who had died the year before.

Jacquline Babbin, who produced *All My Children* during the '80s, has written several murder mysteries with a show-business angle, one of which was titled *Bloody Soaps*.

Louise Shaffer, who as Goldie Kane was involved in a scheme to murder her former stepdaughter Erica, has written murder mysteries with a show-business angle. Her first took place on the set of a fictional soap opera and was titled *All My Suspects*.

The son of a journalist who has written for *The Wall Street Journal*, Roscoe Born (*Jim Thomasen*) has published his own book, *The Suspended Sentence: A Guide for Writers*.

William Mooney (*Paul Martin*) has authored a writing guide, *ASAP: The Fastest Way to Create a Memorable Speech*.

Robin Mattson (*Janet Green*), who hosted her own cooking show, *The Main Ingredient,* on Lifetime, published a cookbook in 1997 titled *Soap Opera Café*.

Walt Willey, a cartoonist, helped script himself into the thirteenth issue of the comic book *The Second Life of Dr. Mirage*. Willey has been friends since childhood with Kim Howard Johnson, who owns Valiant Comics, which publishes *Dr. Mirage*. At her wedding, Willey struck up a conversation with one of the company's artists about the similarities between comic books and soap operas. Before too long, he was sitting down with one of *Dr. Mirage*'s writers, plotting himself into a story in which a cult had targeted him for assassination.

Richard Hatch has written the story for an issue of a comic book based on his old TV series *Battlestar Galactica*.

Walt Willey, Bill Timoney, and Ruth Warrick have all written regular columns for soap opera magazines: Warrick for *Soap Opera Digest*, Timoney for *Soap Opera Weekly*, and Willey for *Soap Opera Update*. Willey also drew and wrote a short-lived comic strip for *Soap Opera Weekly*.

In 1997, Erica Kane penned a guide to life both on and off the show called *Having It All* (Hyperion). *Having It All* was published in hardcover because Erica Kane would not have it any other way.

Fun and Games

The 1985 TSR board game *All My Children* allowed up to six players at a time to step into the shoes of such Pine Valley residents as Erica Kane, Adam Chandler, Greg Nelson, Palmer Cortlandt, Daisy Cortlandt, Brooke English, Phoebe Tyler, Hillary Wilson, Dottie Thornton, Angie Hubbard, Jesse Hubbard, and Tad Martin. Players move around the board to such notable Pine Valley locales as the Glamo-Rama, Cortlandt Manor, and the Pine Cone Motel, where they score points for fulfilling their goal cards. Goals range from seducing Hillary on her birthday to shooting Adam Chandler in the back. The first player to rack up one hundred points fulfilling their goals wins.

Decipher, Inc. manufactured a different sort of roleplaying game for *All My Children* fans. Modeled after murder mystery weekends, Decipher's "How to Host a Murder" kits contained all the necessary ingredients for eight players to act out a murder mystery in their own home. One of the kits in that series borrowed characters from *All My Children*. A plastic surgeon is murdered at the

Valley Inn and suspicion falls on such characters as Erica, Brooke, Jackson, Palmer, and Phoebe. Each of the eight players picks a character, whom they will then play for the rest of the evening as they read through varied documents trying to figure which one of them is the killer.

In the late '80s, United States Playing Card Company manufactured a Trivial Pursuit–style quiz game themed around several daytime soap operas, among them *All My Children*. The game consisted of cards containing six questions each in such categories as romance, family ties, and legal problems. The game included more than three hundred questions about *All My Children*. Although not officially associated with Trivial Pursuit, the question cards could be used with the Trivial Pursuit board and came with a custom-crafted die that featured an icon for each of the six categories on all six faces.

Star Pics issued a collection of *All My Children* trading cards in 1991. The seventy-two-card series featured images of the show's then current cast members as well as varied scenes from the show's history. The backs of the cards detailed characters' biographies, memorable love stories, and behind-the-scenes information. (One card, for example, reports that the makeup department "uses an average of one quart of foundation per month [and] goes through 25 cans of hairspray each month.") The first card in the series belonged, appropriately, to creator Agnes Nixon. A special double-faced subset of the cards was devoted to Erica Kane–Susan Lucci. Some packs contained preview cards from *General Hospital, One Life to Live,* and *Loving* series that were never released.

In 1997, Mattel, the manufacturer of Barbie dolls, announced plans to produce an Erica Kane doll.

Final Exam in
<u>Child</u> Development

(Answers on page 200.)

(1970) What kind of business did Nick Davis open up when he first returned to Pine Valley?
(a) dance studio
(b) beauty salon
(c) modeling agency
(d) pool hall

(1971) What caused Chuck Tyler to collapse during his wedding to Tara Martin?
(a) fatigue
(b) kidney failure
(c) the appearance of a presumed dead Phil Brent
(d) withdrawal from amphetamines

(1972) What medical diagnosis prompted Nick Davis to ask his wife Anne for a divorce?
   (a) Nick learned that he had a low sperm count.
   (b) Nick learned that a fatal blood condition ran in his family.
   (c) Nick learned that Anne could never have children.
   (d) Nick learned that he was dying from a degenerative disease.

(1973) What incident triggered Kitty Shea's bout with depression?
   (a) She was held hostage by Ray Gardner.
   (b) She miscarried Nick Davis's child.
   (c) Lincoln Tyler dumped her for Erica Kane.
   (d) She discovered that Myrtle Fargate was only posing as her mother.

(1974) What did Erica Kane want from Dr. Joe Martin in exchange for testifying on Jeff's behalf during his murder trial?
   (a) the name of a doctor who would perform an abortion for her
   (b) Joe's promise that he would convince Jeff to grant her a divorce
   (c) access to Phil Brent's medical records
   (d) money

(1975) What crime did Kitty Shea's ex-husband Hal
blackmail her into helping him commit?
(a) setting up Phoebe Tyler for blackmail
(b) breaking into Phoebe Tyler's safe
(c) stealing drugs from the hospital
(d) selling drugs through the Boutique

(1976) How did Margo Flax try to kill Ann Tyler, her
rival for Paul Martin's affection?
(a) She locked Ann in the storage room and set
fire to the Boutique.
(b) She poisoned Ann's afternoon cup of tea.
(c) She filled the Boutique with carbon
monoxide.
(d) She walled Ann up in the dressing room at
the Boutique.

(1977) For what crime was Phoebe Tyler sent to
prison?
(a) aiding and abetting a fugitive
(b) perjury
(c) possession of marijuana
(d) drunk driving

(1978) With what drug did Dr. David Thornton poison
his wife Edna's iced tea in the hopes of doing
away with her?
(a) arsenic
(b) belladonna
(c) cyanide
(d) digitalis

(1979) On what holiday was Joey Martin born?
(a) New Year's Day
(b) Mother's Day
(c) Fourth of July
(d) Christmas

(1980) With whom did Devon McFadden cheat on her husband Wally?
(a) Benny Sago
(b) Dan Kennicott
(c) Sean Cudahy
(d) Cliff Warner

(1981) What was the name of the sleazy bar where Jenny Gardner and Jesse Hubbard worked?
(a) Tony's
(b) Foxy's
(c) The Hot Spot
(d) The Lizards' Lounge

(1982) What truth did Liza Colby reveal to Jenny on prom night that sent Jenny running out of town?
(a) Liza had slept with Jenny's boyfriend, Greg Nelson.
(b) Jenny's mother Opal had been carrying on an affair with Langley Wallingford.
(c) Jenny's father had once raped Ruth Martin.
(d) Jenny's brother Tad was sitting in prison for drug possession.

(1983) To what substance did Mark Dalton become
       addicted?
       (a) amphetamines
       (b) barbiturates
       (c) cocaine
       (d) designer drugs

(1984) Why was Cliff Warner's medical license
       suspended?
       (a) He lost a malpractice suit.
       (b) Liza Colby accused him of touching her
           improperly during an examination.
     ✓ (c) He treated his sister Linda's boyfriend for a
           bullet wound and did not report it to the
           police.
       (d) He was accused of pulling the plug on a
           terminally ill patient.

(1985) Natalie Hunter was already married to Jeremy's
       father when the character was introduced, but
       what was her maiden name?
       (a) Durbin
       (b) Green
       (c) Marlowe
       (d) Webb

(1986) After tricking Phoebe into marriage and trying
to kill her, Wade Matthews tried to escape Pine
Valley disguised as what?
(a) a priest
(b) a burn victim
(c) a woman
(d) a police officer

(1987) For what political office was Travis Montgomery
running when he became involved with Erica
Kane?
(a) mayor
(b) governor
(c) senator
(d) district attorney

(1988) How was Jesse Hubbard killed?
(a) He was shot.
(b) His car was forced over the side of a cliff.
(c) He died in an explosion.
(d) He was poisoned.

(1989) Why was Julie Chandler's marriage to Nico
Kelly not valid?
(a) Julie was underage when they exchanged vows.
(b) Nico was still married to Cecily Davidson.
(c) The mayor who married them was not
authorized to perform wedding ceremonies.
(d) Their marriage license had expired the day
before they exchanged vows.

(1990) What color hair did Hayley Vaughn have during
her first few months in town?
  (a) black
  (b) blue
  (c) blond
  (d) blood red

(1991) On what holiday did Jeremy Hunter marry
Ceara Connor?
  (a) Valentine's Day
  (b) Bastille Day
  (c) Christmas Eve
  (d) New Year's Eve

(1992) What caused Natalie Dillon's blindness?
  (a) a fire
  (b) a brain tumor
  (c) a gunshot wound
  (d) stress

(1993) After Laurel Banning killed her ex-husband
Denny in self-defense, what did she and Jackson
Montgomery do with the body?
  (a) They buried it in Erica Kane's backyard.
  (b) They buried in the Marrick family crypt.
  (c) They dumped it in the well where Janet had
       imprisoned Natalie.
  (d) They dumped it in the pond on Palmer
       Cortlandt's estate.

(1994) What family secret did Maria and Edmund discover during their honeymoon in Hungary?
    (a) that Edmund was really Dimitri's half-brother
    (b) that Hugo Marrick had killed Edmund's mother Flora
    (c) that Dimitri and Corvina had been switched at birth, making Corvina the Marick heir
    (d) that Anton Lang was really Dimitri's son

(1995) What screen names did Cecily Davidson and Charlie Brent use while falling in love with each other on the Internet?
    (a) "Love's Fool" and "Lonesome Heart"
    (b) "Clueless" and "Beyond Clueless"
    (c) "Pining Away" and "Valley Girl"
    (d) "Once Bitten" and "Twice Shy"

(1996) How did Dixie find out about Tad's one-night stand with Liza Colby?
    (a) The truth came out in court when Liza sued Tad for sexual harrassment.
    (b) Tad confessed to the affair during a therapy session.
    (c) Marian broadcast an audiotape of Tad and Liza discussing their affair over the sound system at WRCW.
    (d) Dixie read about it in *The National Intruder*.

(1997) Who delivered Edmund and Maria's daughter
Madeleine?
(a) Joe Martin
(b) Gloria Marsh
(c) Erica Kane
(d) Dimitri Marrick

All The Answers

Erica Lucci: (1) b (2) b (3) c (4) a (5) d (6) a (7) b (8) c (9) a (10) b (11) d (12) c

(Photo Bonus) After jumping bail, Erica dressed as a nun so she could sneak into the funeral for Kent Bogard, the ex-lover she had been arrested for murdering.

The Love Connection: (1) b (2) a (3) c (4) b (5) c (6) a (7) d (8) b (9) d (10) c (11) b (12) a (13) d (14) b (15) d

Pine Valley's Ten Most Wanted List: (1) Ray Gardner (2) Billy Clyde Tuggle (3) Peg English (4) Dr. Jonathan Kinder (5) Louis Greco (6) Damon Lazarre (7) Carter Jones (8) Lars Bogard (9) Wade Matthews (10) Richard Fields

Pre-*Child*hood: (1) f (2) g (3) l (4) c (5) h (6) k (7) b (8) i (9) d (10) e (11) j (12) a

The Graduates: (1) f (2) e (3) d (4) g (5) h (6) a (7) j (8) c (9) b (10) i

Final Exam in *Child* Development: (1970) a (1971) b (1972) a (1973) b (1974) d (1975) d (1976) c (1977) d (1978) d (1979) d (1980) c (1981) b (1982) c (1983) c (1984) c (1985) c (1986) c (1987) c (1988) a (1989) c (1990) a (1991) d (1992) a (1993) c (1994) d (1995) b (1996) c (1997) c

Index

Character names are in **boldface**. Page numbers in *italics* refer to picture captions.

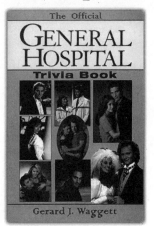